PROPOSALS

In the same series

Feasts: an anthology
selected and edited by
Christopher Bland and Linda Kelly

PROPOSALS

A lovers' anthology

EDITED BY
Laurence and Linda Kelly

Constable · London

First published in Great Britain 1989
by Constable and Company Limited
10 Orange Street London WC2H 7EG
Copyright © Laurence and Linda Kelly 1989
Set in Linotron Bembo 11 pt by
Rowland Phototypesetting Limited
Bury St Edmunds, Suffolk
Printed in Great Britain by
St Edmundsbury Press Limited
Bury St Edmunds, Suffolk

British Library CIP data
Proposals: a lovers' anthology
1. Literature. Special subjects. Love.
Anthologies
I. Kelly, Laurence   II. Kelly, Linda, *1936–*
808.8'0354

ISBN 0 09 468880 X

TO BEN AND SARA

Contents

Acknowledgements	11
Introduction	13

PUTTING THE QUESTION

Placetne magistra? – *Gaudy Night*, Dorothy L. Sayers	17
Bernard and Ethel – *The Young Visiters*, Daisy Ashford	18
A modest proposal – Jonathan Swift to Jane Waring	21
Something rather sweet – *Decline and Fall*, Evelyn Waugh	22
Tolstoy's letter – Countess Tolstoy's diary, translated by P. Snelling	23
What's in a name? – *The Importance of being Earnest*, Oscar Wilde	25
A bit of spirit – *Family Memories*, Rebecca West	27
In brief – *Summer Lightning*, P. G. Wodehouse	28

WORLDLY CONSIDERATIONS

The Duke and Zuleika – *Zuleika Dobson*, Max Beerbohm	31
Becky loses her baronet – *Vanity Fair*, William Makepeace Thackeray	36
Madame Goesler's generosity – *Phineas Finn*, Anthony Trollope	38
A question of the dowry – *The Paston Letters*	44
A left and a right – *The Sixth Great Power*, Philip Ziegler	45

LOVE AT FIRST SIGHT

Slava's courtship – *Galina*, Galina Vishnevskaya, translated by Guy Daniels	49
Heart struck – *The Happy Hypocrite*, Max Beerbohm	53

Contents

Oroonoko and Imoinda – *Oroonoko*, Aphra Behn ... 56
A look before leaping – *Brief Lives*, John Aubrey ... 58

UNWELCOME APPROACHES

Blood bond – *Nightmare Abbey*, Thomas Love Peacock ... 61
Filing a declaration – *Bleak House*, Charles Dickens ... 62
Mr Collins proposes – *Pride and Prejudice*, Jane Austen ... 66

HIGH ROMANCE

Under the moon – *The Ordeal of Richard Feverel*, George Meredith ... 73
Lord Orville declares himself – *Evelina*, Fanny Burney ... 74
Linda and Fabrice – *The Pursuit of Love*, Nancy Mitford ... 75
In the orchard – *Jane Eyre*, Charlotte Brontë ... 78
Balcony scene – *Romeo and Juliet*, William Shakespeare ... 89

HURT FEELINGS

Tom and Becky – *Tom Sawyer*, Mark Twain ... 93
Disraeli's remonstrance – Benjamin Disraeli to Mary Anne Wyndham Lewis ... 96
Lord Reggie is offended – *The Green Carnation*, Robert Hitchens ... 98

FAIRY-TALE AND FANTASY

Under the lee of the diamond mountain – *The Diamond as big as the Ritz*, F. Scott Fitzgerald ... 105
The fairy ring – *The Rose and the Ring*, William Makepeace Thackeray ... 106
The courtship of the Yonghy-Bonghy-Bo – Edward Lear ... 110
The Top and the Ball – *Danish Fairy-tales and Legends*, Hans Andersen ... 113

ROYAL REQUESTS

Victoria and Albert – Queen Victoria's journal ... 119
Henry VIII and Mary of Guise – *Mary of Guise*, Rosalind K. Marshall ... 119

Contents

Henry V woos Katharine of France – *Henry V*, William
Shakespeare ... 121
Advances to Attila – *The Decline and Fall of the Roman Empire*,
Edward Gibbon ... 125

PROXY PROPOSALS

Barkis is willin' – *David Copperfield*, Charles Dickens ... 129
Bertie speaks for Gussie – *Right ho, Jeeves*, P. G. Wodehouse ... 131

RECONCILIATIONS AND REUNIONS

Gabriel and Bathsheba – *Far from the Madding Crowd*, Thomas
Hardy ... 143
Below stairs – *Kipps*, H. G. Wells ... 147
Captain Wentworth's letter – *Persuasion*, Jane Austen ... 151
Shipboard romance – *The Baker's Dozen*, Saki ... 152
No shadow of another parting – *Great Expectations*, Charles
Dickens ... 157

PROPOSITIONS

The passionate shepherd to his love – Christopher Marlowe ... 163
The nymph's reply – Walter Raleigh ... 164
Setting out the alternatives – *The Charterhouse of Parma*,
Stendhal, translated by C. K. Scott Moncrieff ... 165
Struck by the dart of love – Henry VIII to Anne Boleyn ... 167
Not to be forgotten – Claire Clairmont to Lord Byron ... 168
No words wasted – *Love Letters*, Antonia Fraser ... 169

REJECTIONS AND REFUSALS

Sarah, Duchess of Marlborough refuses the Duke of
Somerset ... 173
The wrong approach – *Return to Yesterday*, Ford Madox Ford ... 173
Patrick Brontë and Mary Burder ... 174
Tatyana and Onegin – *Eugene Onegin*, Alexander Pushkin,
translated by Charles Johnston ... 178
Judy and Roddy – *Dusty Answer*, Rosamund Lehmann ... 188

Contents

BREACH OF PROMISE

Complications – *Dr Smart-Allick at Narkover*, Beachcomber (J. B. Morton)	195
mehitabel has an adventure – *archy and mehitabel*, Don Marquis	197

HAPPY ENDINGS

Pulling together – *Good Wives*, Louisa M. Alcott	203
A business arrangement – *North and South*, Elizabeth Gaskell	204
Among the primroses – *Henry and Cato*, Iris Murdoch	207
Spelling it out – *Anna Karenina*, Leo Tolstoy, translated by Constance Garnett	209
Love on the hunting-field – *Mr Sponge's Sporting Tour*, R. S. Surtees	211
The simplest pattern – *Of Human Bondage*, W. Somerset Maugham	215
No longer alone – *Castle Gay*, John Buchan	219
Molly Bloom's soliloquy – *Ulysses*, James Joyce	220

Acknowledgements

We are grateful to the following for permission to quote from their works, editions or translations:

Hodder & Stoughton for Dorothy L. Sayers' *Gaudy Night*; Penguin Books for Evelyn Waugh's *Decline and Fall*; Virago for Rebecca West's *Family Memories*; A. P. Watt Ltd on behalf of the Trustees of the Wodehouse Trust for P. G. Wodehouse's *Summer Lightning*; Collins and Philip Ziegler for *The Sixth Great Power*: Hodder & Stoughton for *Galina* by Galina Vishnevskaya, translated by Guy Daniels; Mrs Eva Reichmann for *The Happy Hypocrite* by Max Beerbohm; the Peters Fraser & Dunlop Group Ltd for Nancy Mitford's *The Pursuit of Love*; Century Hutchinson for P. G. Wodehouse's *Right ho, Jeeves*: Bodley Head for F. Scott Fitzgerald's *The Diamond as big as the Ritz*; Collins for Rosalind K. Marshall's *Mary of Guise*; A. P. Watt Ltd on behalf of the Literary Executors of the Estate of H. G. Wells for *Kipps* by H. G. Wells; Weidenfeld & Nicolson for *Love Letters* by Antonia Fraser; The Society of Authors and Miss Rosamond Lehmann for *Dusty Answer*; Express Newspapers plc for *Dr Smart-Allick at Narkover* by Beachcomber (J. B. Morton); Faber and Faber for Don Marquis's *archy and mehitabel*: Iris Murdoch and Chatto and Windus for *Henry and Cato*; William Heinemann Ltd for W. Somerset Maugham's *Of Human Bondage* and Max Beerbohm's *Zuleika Dobson*; Bodley Head for James Joyce's *Ulysses*; Gollancz for Countess Tolstoy's diary, translated by P. Snelling; Hodder & Stoughton for John Buchan's *Castle Gay*; University of Nebraska Press for Robert Hitchens's *The Green Carnation*; David Higham for Ford Madox Ford's *Return to Yesterday*: and Penguin for Sir Charles Johnston's translation of *Eugene Onegin* by A. Pushkin.

We would also like to thank the Bridgeman Art Library for

Acknowledgements

permission to reproduce 'The Lovers' by Renoir, which appears on the jacket; and to Marina Berry, Jenny Bland, David Clement-Davies, Harriet Cullen, Sebastian Grigg, Mollie Philipps, Antonia Pinter, Sarah Skinner, John Train, and our three children for their help, suggestions, and encouragement.

L.K.
L.K.
1989

Introduction

Every marriage and indeed love affair begins with a proposal. It may be spoken or unspoken, romantic or matter of fact, but in one way or another a question has been asked and answered. Few people forget such moments in their lives.

The proposals – and sometimes propositions – here have been chosen with no other criterion than their power to move or entertain. Most come from fiction, though not that section of romantic literature through which, as Rebecca West once put it, the galloping hoofs of the Tosh horse can be heard. Some are so famous as to be literary touchstones, but how can one compose an anthology of proposals without including Mr Rochester's to Jane Eyre or Mr Collins's to Elizabeth Bennet?

Marriage is a contract and behind the fine words of a proposal a bargain is often being struck, with wealth and rank as definite considerations. Becky Sharp weeps with disappointment at missing the chance of marrying a baronet, decrepit and old as he is. Phineas Finn is tempted not only by Madame Goesler's charm and beauty but by the political future her money can offer. Disraeli, in his passionate remonstrance to Mrs Wyndham Lewis – which led to her accepting him – admits that her fortune had first been an attraction.

The Duke of Dorset is all too conscious of the differences in their stations when he proposes to Zuleika Dobson. But her response to his lyrical enumeration of his titles and possessions is satisfyingly robust: 'I think you are an awful snob.'

This spirited indifference to worldly advantages, the reverse side of the bargaining coin, is seen in Harriet Vane's resistance to Lord Peter Wimsey. Not only is he the son of a duke, rich and charming, he has also saved her from a conviction for murder. Pride, and a

Introduction

sense of obligation, keep the two apart for several novels till the spell of Oxford at last brings them together.

As a general principle, at least on the evidence of this anthology, a woman who proposes to a man is likely to be humiliated. The shame which Tatyana experiences after writing to Eugene Onegin is echoed in Rosamund Lehmann's *Dusty Answer* when Judith declares her love for Roddy. (Both episodes prove the point that it is a mistake to write love letters late at night.) Only Queen Victoria emerges unscathed from such a situation. Royal etiquette compels her to speak first but the outcome makes her 'the happiest of human beings'.

Another type of wooer is the one who pleads another's cause. Cyrano de Bergerac is the most obvious example but Rostand's verses lose in translation and we have regretfully omitted Cyrano's moonlight wooing of Roxane. Touched by the same chivalrous spirit – but not, like Cyrano, in love with the girl in question – is Bertie Wooster when he takes it on himself to speak for Gussie Fink-Nottle. His narrow escape at the end of this episode will not be the last of the matter. The Bassett menace will recur.

Sometimes infatuation takes the place of passion. Claire Clairmont flings herself at Byron's head on the slightest of acquaintanceships and brings him vividly before our eyes: 'I shall ever remember the gentleness of your manners and the wild originality of your countenance.' Sometimes the refusal is more memorable than the question. Who can forget the Duchess of Marlborough's splendid response to the Duke of Somerset, or Marie of Guise's to Henry VIII: 'I may be big in person but my neck is small'? But there are sufficient acceptances here as well, Molly Bloom's ecstatic 'yes' among them, to reassure us that true love is perennial and that however customs and conventions vary the happiest journeys end in lovers meeting.

Putting the Question

Placetne, Magistra?

The final Chorale was sung, and the audience made their way out. Harriet's way lay through the Broad Street gate; Peter followed through the quad.

'It's a beautiful night – far too good to waste. Don't go back yet. Come down to Magdalen Bridge and send your love to London River.'

They turned along the Broad in silence, the light wind fluttering their gowns as they walked.

'There's something about this place,' said Peter presently, 'that alters one's values.' He paused, and added a little abruptly: 'I have said a good deal to you one way and another, lately; but you may have noticed that since we came to Oxford I have not asked you to marry me.'

'Yes,' said Harriet, her eyes fixed upon the severe and delicate silhouette of the Bodleian roof, just emerging between the Sheldonian and Clarendon Building. 'I had noticed it.'

'I have been afraid,' he said simply; 'because I knew that from anything you said to me here, there could be no going back . . . But I will ask you now, and if you say No, I promise you that this time I will accept your answer. Harriet; you know that I love you: will you marry me?'

The traffic lights winked at the Holywell Corner: Yes; No; Wait. Cat Street was crossed and the shadows of New College walls had swallowed them up before she spoke:

'Tell me one thing, Peter. Will it make you desperately unhappy if I say No?'

'Desperately? . . . My dear, I will not insult either you or myself with a word like that. I can only tell you that if you will marry me it will give me very great happiness.'

Putting the Question

They passed beneath the arch of the bridge and out into the pale light once more.

'Peter!'

She stood still; and he stopped perforce and turned towards her. She laid both hands upon the fronts of his gown, looking into his face while she searched for the word that should carry her over the last difficult breach.

It was he who found it for her. With a gesture of submission he bared his head and stood gravely, the square cap dangling in his hand.

'Placetne, magistra?'

'Placet.'

The Proctor, stumping grimly past with averted eyes, reflected that Oxford was losing all sense of dignity. But what could he do? If Senior Members of the University chose to stand – in their gowns, too! – closely and passionately embracing in New College Lane right under the Warden's windows, he was powerless to prevent it. He primly settled his white band and went upon his walk unheeded; and no hand plucked his velvet sleeve.

Dorothy L. Sayers: *Gaudy Night*

Bernard and Ethel

Next morning while imbibing his morning tea beneath his pink silken quilt Bernard decided he must marry Ethel with no more delay. I love the girl he said to himself and she must be mine but I somehow feel I can not propose in London it would not be seemly in the city of London. We must go for a day in the country and when surrounded by the gay twittering of the birds and the smell of the cows I will lay my suit at her feet and he waved his arm wildly at the gay thought. Then he sprang from bed and gave a rat tat at Ethel's door.

Putting the Question

Are you up my dear he called.

Well not quite said Ethel hastilly jumping from her downy nest.

Be quick cried Bernard I have a plan to spend a day near Windsor Castle and we will take our lunch and spend a happy day.

Oh Hurrah shouted Ethel I shall soon be ready as I had my bath last night so wont wash very much now.

No dont said Bernard and added in a rarther fervent tone through the chink of the door you are fresher than the rose my dear no soap could make you fairer.

Then he dashed off very embarrased to dress. Ethel blushed and felt a bit excited as she heard the words and she put on a new white muslin dress in a fit of high spirits. She looked very beautifull with some red roses in her hat and the dainty red ruge in her cheeks looked quite the thing. Bernard heaved a sigh and his eyes flashed as he beheld her and Ethel thought to herself what a fine type of manhood he reprisented with his nice thin legs in pale broun trousers and well fitting spats and a red rose in his button hole and rarther a sporting cap which gave him a great air with its quaint check and little flaps to pull down if necessary. Off they started the envy of all the waiters.

They arrived at Windsor very hot from the journey and Bernard at once hired a boat to row his beloved up the river. Ethel could not row but she much enjoyed seeing the tough sunburnt arms of Barnard tugging at the oars as she lay among the rich cushons of the dainty boat. She had a rarther lazy nature but Bernard did not know of this. However he soon got dog tired and sugested lunch by the mossy bank.

Oh yes said Ethel quickly opening the sparkling champaigne.

Dont spill any cried Bernard as he carved some chicken.

They eat and drank deeply of the charming viands ending up with merangs and choclates.

Let us now bask under the spreading trees said Bernard in a passiunate tone.

Oh yes lets said Ethel and she opened her dainty parasole and sank down upon the long green grass. She closed her eyes but she was far from asleep. Bernard sat beside her in profound silence gazing at her pink face and long wavy eye lashes. He puffed at his pipe for some

Putting the Question

moments while the larks gaily caroled in the blue sky. Then he edged a trifle closer to Ethels form.

Ethel he murmered in a trembly voice.

Oh what is it said Ethel hastily sitting up.

Words fail me ejaculated Bernard horsly my passion for you is intense he added fervently. It has grown day and night since I first beheld you.

Oh said Ethel in supprise I am not prepared for this and she lent back against the trunk of the tree.

Bernard placed on arm tightly round her. When will you marry me Ethel he uttered you must be my wife it has come to that I love you so intensely that if you say no I shall perforce dash my body to the brink of yon muddy river he panted wildly.

Oh dont do that implored Ethel breathing rarther hard.

Then say you love me he cried.

Oh Bernard she sighed fervently I certinly love you madly you are to me like a Heathen god she cried looking at his manly form and handsome flashing face I will indeed marry you.

How soon gasped Bernard gazing at her intensely.

As soon as possible said Ethel gently closing her eyes.

My Darling whispered Bernard and he seiezed her in his arms we will be marrid next week.

Oh Bernard muttered Ethel this is so sudden.

No no cried Bernard and taking the bull by both horns he kissed her violently on her dainty face. My bride to be he murmered several times.

Ethel trembled with joy as she heard the mistick words.

Oh Bernard she said little did I ever dream of such as this and she suddenly fainted into his out stretched arms.

Oh I say gasped Bernard and laying the dainty burden on the grass he dashed to the waters edge and got a cup full of the fragrant river to pour on his true loves pallid brow.

She soon came to and looked up with a sickly smile Take me back to the Gaierty hotel she whispered faintly.

With plesure my darling said Bernard I will just pack up our viands ere I unloose the boat.

Ethel felt better after a few drops of champagne and began to tidy her hair while Bernard packed the remains of the food. Then arm in arm they tottered to the boat.

I trust you have not got an illness my darling murmered Bernard as he helped her in.

Oh no I am very strong said Ethel I fainted from joy she added to explain matters.

Oh I see said Bernard handing her a cushon well some people do he added kindly and so saying they rowed down the dark stream now flowing silently beneath a gold moon. All was silent as the lovers glided home with joy in their hearts and radiunce on their faces only the sound of the mystearious water lapping against the frail vessel broke the monotony of the night.

So I will end my chapter.

Daisy Ashford: *The Young Visiters*

A modest proposal

Dublin, 1700.
Are you in a condition to manage domestic affairs with an income of less than three hundred pounds a year? Have you such an inclination to my person and honour as to comply with my desires and way of living, and endeavour to make us both as happy as you can? Will you be ready to engage in those methods I shall direct for the improvement of your mind, so as to make us entertaining company for each other, without being miserable when we are neither visiting nor visited? Can you bend your love and esteem and indifference to others the same way as I do mine? Shall I have so much power in your heart, or you so much government of your passions as to grow in good humour upon my approach though provoked by a—? Have you so much good nature as to endeavour by soft words to smooth any ragged humour occasioned by the cross accidents of life? Shall the place wherever your husband is thrown be more welcome than courts or cities without him? In short, these

are some of the necessary methods to please men who, like me, are deep-read in the world; and to a person thus made, I should be proud in giving all due returns towards making her happy. These are the questions I have always resolved to propose to her with whom I meant to pass my life; and whenever you can heartily answer them in the affirmative, I shall be blessed to have you in my arms, without regarding whether your person be beautiful or your fortune large. Cleanliness in the first and competence in the second is all I look for.

Jonathan Swift to Jane Waring

Something rather sweet

At dinner Margot talked about matters of daily interest, about some jewels she was having reset, and how they had come back all wrong; and how all the wiring of her London house was being overhauled because of the fear of fire; and how the man she had left in charge of her villa at Cannes had made a fortune at the Casino and given her notice, and she was afraid she might have to go out there to arrange about it; and how the Society for the Preservation of Ancient Buildings was demanding a guarantee that she would not demolish her castle in Ireland; and how her cook seemed to be going off his head that night, the dinner was so dull; and how Bobby Pastmaster was trying to borrow money from her again, on the grounds that she had misled him when she bought his house and that if he had known she was going to pull it down he would have made her pay more. 'Which is not logical of Bobby,' she said. 'The less I valued this house, the less I ought to have paid, surely? Still, I'd better send him something, otherwise he'll go and marry, and I think it may be nice for Peter to have the title when he grows up.'

Later, when they were alone, she said: 'People talk a great deal of nonsense about being rich. Of course it is a bore in some ways, and it means endless work, but I wouldn't be poor, or even moderately well-off, for all the ease in the world. Would you be happy if you were rich, do you think?'

'Well, it depends how I got the money,' said Paul.

'I don't see how that comes in.'

'No, I don't quite mean that. What I mean is that I think there's only one thing that could make me really happy, and if I got that I should be rich too, but it wouldn't matter being rich, you see, because, however rich I was, and I hadn't got what would make me happy, I shouldn't be happy, you see.'

'My precious, that's rather obscure,' said Margot, 'but I think it may mean something rather sweet.' He looked up at her, and her eyes met his unfalteringly. 'If it does, I'm glad,' she added.

'Margot, darling, beloved, please, will you marry me?' Paul was on his knees by her chair, his hands on hers.

'Well, that's rather what I've been wanting to discuss with you all day.' But surely there was a tremor in her voice?

'Does that mean that possibly you might, Margot? Is there a chance that you will?'

'I don't see why not. Of course we must ask Peter about it, and there are other things we ought to discuss first,' and then, quite suddenly, 'Paul, dear, dear creature, come here.'

Evelyn Waugh: Decline and Fall

Tolstoy's letter

I seized the letter and rushed downstairs into the girls' room, which the three of us shared. Here is the letter:

'Sophine Andreyevna, it is becoming unbearable. For three weeks I've been saying to myself: "I shall tell her now" and yet I continue to go away with the same feeling of sadness, regret, terror, and happiness in my heart. Every night I go over the past and curse myself for not having spoken to you, and wonder what I would have said if I *had* spoken. I am taking this letter with me in order to

Putting the Question

hand it to you should my courage fail me again. Your family have the false notion, I believe, that I am in love with Lisa. This is quite wrong . . . At Ivitsy I might still have been able to break away and to return to my hermitage, back to my solitary work and my absorbing labours. Now I can't do anything; I feel I have created a disturbance in your home, and that your friendship for me, as a good, honourable man, has also been spoiled. I dare not leave and I dare not stay. You are a candid, honest girl; with your hand on your heart, and without hurrying (for God's sake, don't hurry!), tell me what to do. I would have laughed myself sick a month ago if I had been told that I would suffer, suffer joyfully, as I have been doing for this past month. Tell me, with all the candour that is yours: Will you be my wife? If you can say *yes, boldly*, with all your heart, then *say it*; but if you have the faintest shadow of doubt, say *no*. For heaven's sake, think it over carefully. I am terrified to think of a *no*, but I am prepared for it and will be strong enough to bear it. But it will be terrible if I am not loved by my wife as much as I love you!'

I didn't read the letter carefully, I merely skipped over it till I reached the words, 'Will you be my wife?' I was going to return upstairs and say yes to Lev Nikolaevich, when I ran into Lisa, who asked me: 'Well?'

'Le comte m'a fait la proposition,' I answered quickly. Mother came in then, and realised at once what had happened. She took me firmly by the shoulders and, turning my face to the door, she said, 'Go and give him your answer.'

I flew up the stairs, as light as a feather, and, rushing past the dining-room and drawing-room, I flew into my mother's bedroom. Lev Nikolaevich stood in the corner, leaning against the wall, waiting for me. I went up to him, and he took me by both hands.

'Well?' he asked.

'Of course – yes,' I replied.

A few minutes later everybody in the house knew what had happened, and began to congratulate us.

Countess Tolstoy's diary, 17 September 1862, translated by P. Snelling

What's in a name?

Jack: Charming day it has been, Miss Fairfax.

Gwendolen: Pray don't talk to me about the weather, Mr Worthing. Whenever people talk to me about the weather, I always feel quite certain that they mean something else. And that makes me so nervous.

Jack: I do mean something else.

Gwendolen: I thought so. In fact, I am never wrong.

Jack: And I would like to be allowed to take advantage of Lady Bracknell's temporary absence . . .

Gwendolen: I would certainly advise you to do so. Mamma has a way of coming back suddenly into a room that I have often had to speak to her about.

Jack (*nervously*): Miss Fairfax, ever since I met you I have admired you more than any girl . . . I have ever met since . . . I met you.

Gwendolen: Yes, I am quite well aware of the fact. And I often wish that in public, at any rate, you had been more demonstrative. For me you have always had an irresistible fascination. Even before I met you I was far from indifferent to you. (*Jack looks at her in amazement.*) We live, as I hope you know, Mr Worthing, in an age of ideals. The fact is constantly mentioned in the more expensive monthly magazines, and has now reached the provincial pulpits, I am told; and my ideal has always been to love some one of the name of Ernest. There is something in that name that inspires absolute confidence. The moment Algernon first mentioned to me that he had a friend called Ernest, I knew I was destined to love you.

Jack: You really love me, Gwendolen?

Gwendolen: Passionately!

Jack: Darling! You don't know how happy you've made me.

Gwendolen: My own Ernest!

Putting the Question

Jack: But you don't really mean to say that you couldn't love me if my name wasn't Ernest?

Gwendolen: But your name is Ernest.

Jack: Yes, I know it is. But supposing it was something else? Do you mean to say you couldn't love me then?'

Gwendolen (*glibly*): Ah! that is clearly a metaphysical speculation, and like most metaphysical speculations has very little reference at all to the actual facts of real life, as we know them.

Jack: Personally, darling, to speak quite candidly, I don't much care about the name of Ernest . . . I don't think the name suits me at all.

Gwendolen: It suits you perfectly. It is a divine name. It has a music of its own. It produces vibrations.

Jack: Well, really, Gwendolen, I must say that I think there are lots of other much nicer names. I think Jack, for instance, a charming name.

Gwendolen: Jack? . . . No, there is very little music in the name Jack, if any at all, indeed. It does not thrill. It produces absolutely no vibrations . . . I have known several Jacks, and they all, without exception, were more than usually plain. Besides, Jack is a notorious domesticity of John! And I pity any woman who is married to a man called John. She would probably never be allowed to know the entrancing pleasure of a single moment's solitude. The only really safe name is Ernest.

Jack: Gwendolen, I must get christened at once – I mean we must get married at once. There is no time to be lost.

Gwendolen: Married, Mr Worthing?

Jack (*astounded*): Well . . . surely. You know that I love you, and you led me to believe, Miss Fairfax, that you were not absolutely indifferent to me.

Gwendolen: I adore you. But you haven't proposed to me yet. Nothing has been said at all about marriage. The subject has not even been touched on.

Jack: Well . . . may I propose to you now?

Gwendolen: I think it would be an admirable opportunity. And to spare you any possible disappointment, Mr Worthing, I think it only fair to tell you quite frankly beforehand that I am fully determined to accept you.

Putting the Question

Jack: Gwendolen!
Gwendolen: Yes, Mr Worthing, what have you got to say to me?
Jack: You know what I have got to say to you.
Gwendolen: Yes, but you don't say it.
Jack: Gwendolen, will you marry me? (*Goes on his knees.*)
Gwendolen: Of course I will, darling. How long you have been about it! I am afraid you have had very little experience in how to propose.
Jack: My own one, I have never loved any one in the world but you.
Gwendolen: Yes, but men often propose for practice. I know my brother Gerald does. All my girl-friends tell me so. What wonderfully blue eyes you have, Ernest! They are quite, quite blue. I hope you will always look at me just like that, especially when there are other people present.

Oscar Wilde: *The Importance of Being Earnest*

A bit of spirit

Presently the ship on which my mother was supposed to make her return journey to England was back from its special commission and reported as ready to make the homeward journey in a fortnight's time. Charles Fairfield heard the news on the same day as my mother. Ever since that day at the riverside hotel, he had been calling more frequently than before at the Mullins' hotel to sit with them on a shadowed balcony, watching the sun set over the bay behind a frieze of prodigal trees growing in their neighbour's garden and drinking fruit juices which Mrs Mullins had bottled and kept in the cisterns sunk by the farmers who had first built the house; and Mrs Mullins would go and fetch my mother to join them, and she would come in, wearing a cool thin dress. These evenings must have given perfect satisfaction to my father's taste. He liked women to be of the neat and slender kind, and the fruit juices were also exactly what he liked: he hated the taste of alcohol. It touches my heart that my mother must certainly have taken his dislike for drink as proof that any woman who married him was bound to be happy. When my father entered the shaded balcony and heard the news of my mother's imminent departure, he greeted the news with an animal sound. 'He uttered one roar, like a bull,' she told us, 'I did not know where to look.'

'Why, Charles!' exclaimed Mrs Mullins, shocked and pleased, and her husband chuckled, 'That's right, Charles, show a bit of spirit, don't let a first-rate filly bolt out of the paddock.'

'You will not sail to England that day,' my father told my mother, rather as if he wished to beat her instead of marry her, which was, as he then announced, his intention.

Rebecca West: Family Memories

In brief

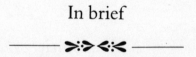

'Ronnie sort of grunted and said "I say!" and I said "Hullo?" and he said "Will you marry me?" and I said "All right," and he said "I ought to warn you, I despise all women," and I said "And I loathe all men" and he said "Right-ho, I think we shall be very happy."'

P. G. Wodehouse: Summer Lightning

Worldly Considerations

The Duke and Zuleika

Luncheon passed in almost unbroken silence. Both Zuleika and the Duke were ravenously hungry, as people always are after the stress of any great emotional crisis. Between them, they made very short work of a cold chicken, a salad, a gooseberry-tart and a Camembert. The Duke filled his glass again and again. The cold classicism of his face had been routed by the new romantic movement which had swept over his soul. He looked two or three months older than when first I showed him to my reader.

He drank his coffee at one draught, pushed back his chair, threw away the cigarette he had just lit. 'Listen!' he said.

Zuleika folded her hands on her lap.

'You do not love me. I accept as final your hint that you never will love me. I need not say – could not, indeed, ever say – how deeply, deeply you have pained me. As lover, I am rejected. But that rejection,' he continued, striking the table, 'is no stopper to my suit. It does but drive me to the use of arguments. My pride shrinks from them. Love, however, is greater than pride; and I, John, Albert, Edward, Claude, Orde, Angus, Tankerton,★ Tanville-Tankerton,† fourteenth Duke of Dorset, Marquis of Dorset, Earl of Grove, Earl of Chastermaine, Viscount Brewsby, Baron Grove, Baron Petstrap, and Baron Wolock, in the Peerage of England, offer you my hand. Do not interrupt me. Do not toss your head. Consider well what I am saying. Weigh the advantages you would gain by acceptance of my hand. Indeed, they are manifold and tremendous. They are also obvious: do not shut your eyes to them. You, Miss Dobson, what are you? A conjurer, and a vagrant;

★ Pronounced as Tacton.
† Pronounced as Tavvle-Tacton.

without means, save such as you can earn by the sleight of your hand; without position; without a home; all unguarded but by your own self-respect. That you follow an honourable calling, I do not for one moment deny. I do, however, ask you to consider how great are its perils and hardships, its fatigues and inconveniences. From all these evils I offer you instant refuge. I offer you, Miss Dobson, a refuge more glorious and more augustly gilded than you, in your airiest flights of fancy, can ever have hoped for or imagined. I own about 340,000 acres. My town-residence is in St James's Square. Tankerton, of which you may have seen photographs, is the chief of my country-seats. It is a Tudor house, set on the ridge of a valley. The valley, its park, is halved by a stream so narrow that the deer leap across. The gardens are estraded upon the slope. Round the house runs a wide paven terrace. There are always two or three peacocks trailing their sheathed feathers along the balustrade, and stepping how stiffly! as though they had just been unharnessed from Juno's chariot. Two flights of shallow steps lead down to the flowers and fountains. Oh, the gardens are wonderful. There is a Jacobean garden of white roses. Between the ends of two pleached alleys, under a dome of branches, is a little lake, with a Triton of black marble, and with waterlilies. Hither and thither under the archipelago of water-lilies, dart gold-fish – tongues of flame in the dark water. There is also a long strait alley of clipped yew. It ends in an alcove for a pagoda of painted porcelain which the Prince Regent – peace be to his ashes! – presented to my great-grandfather. There are many twisting paths, and sudden aspects, and devious, fantastic arbours. Are you fond of horses? In my stables of pinewood and plated-silver seventy are installed. Not all of them together could vie in power with one of the meanest of my motor-cars.'

'Oh, I never go in motors,' said Zuleika. 'They make one look like nothing on earth, and like everybody else.'

'I myself,' said the Duke, 'use them little for that very reason. Are you interested in farming? At Tankerton there is a model farm which would at any rate amuse you, with its heifers and hens and pigs that are like so many big new toys. There is a tiny dairy, which is called "Her Grace's." You could make, therein, real butter with your own hands, and round it into little pats, and press every pat

Worldly Considerations

with a different device. The boudoir that would be yours is a blue room. Four Watteaus hang in it. In the dining-hall hang portraits of my forefathers – *in petto*, your forefathers-in-law – by many masters. Are you fond of peasants? My tenantry are delightful creatures, and there is not one of them who remembers the bringing of the news of the Battle of Waterloo. When a new Duchess is brought to Tankerton, the oldest elm in the park must be felled. That is one of many strange old customs. As she is driven through the village, the children of the tenantry must strew the road with daisies. The bridal chamber must be lighted with as many candles as years have elapsed since the creation of the Dukedom. If you came into it, there would be' – and the youth, closing his eyes, made a rapid calculation – 'exactly three hundred and eighty-eight candles. On the eve of the death of a Duke of Dorset, two black owls come and perch on the battlements. They remain there through the night, hooting. At dawn they fly away, none knows whither. On the eve of the death of any other Tanville-Tankerton, comes (no matter what be the time of year) a cuckoo. It stays for an hour, cooing, then flies away, none knows whither. Whenever this portent occurs, my steward telegraphs to me, that I, as head of the family, be not unsteeled against the shock of a bereavement, and that my authority be sooner given for the unsealing and garnishing of the family-vault. Not every forefather of mine rests quiet beneath his escutcheoned marble. There are they who revisit, in their wrath or their remorse, the places wherein erst they suffered or wrought evil. There is one who, every Halloween, flits into the dining-hall, and hovers before the portrait which Hans Holbein made of him, and flings his diaphanous grey form against the canvas, hoping, maybe, to catch from it the fiery flesh-tints and the solid limbs that were his, and so to be re-incarnate. He flies against the painting, only to find himself t'other side of the wall it hangs on. There are five ghosts permanently residing in the right wing of the house, two in the left, and eleven in the park. But all are quite noiseless and quite harmless. My servants, when they meet them in the corridors or on the stairs, stand aside to let them pass, thus paying them the respect due to guests of mine; but not even the rawest housemaid ever screams or flees at sight of them. I, their host, often waylay them and try to commune with them; but always they glide past me. And how gracefully they glide, these ghosts! It is a pleasure to watch them. It is a lesson in deportment. May they never be laid! Of all my household-pets, they are the dearest to me. I am Duke of Strathsporran and Cairngorm, Marquis of Sorby, and Earl Cairngorm, in the Peerage of Scotland. In the glens of the hills about Strathsporran are many noble and nimble stags. But I have never set foot in my house there, for it is carpeted throughout with the tartan of my clan. You seem to like tartan. What tartan is it you are wearing?'

Zuleika looked down at her skirt. 'I don't know,' she said. 'I got it in Paris.'

'Well,' said the Duke, 'it is very ugly. The Dalbraith tartan is harmonious in comparison, and has, at least, the excuse of history. If you married me, you would have the right to wear it. You would have many strange and fascinating rights. You would go to Court. I admit that the Hanoverian Court is not much. Still, it is better than nothing. At your presentation, moreover, you would be given the *entrée*. Is that nothing to you? You would be driven to Court in my state-coach. It is swung so high that the streetsters can hardly see its occupant. It is lined with rose-silk; and on its panels, and on its hammer-cloth, my arms are emblazoned – no one has ever been able to count the quarterings. You would be wearing the family-jewels, reluctantly surrendered to you by my aunt. They are many and marvellous, in their antique settings. I don't want to brag. It humiliates me to speak to you as I am speaking. But I am heart-set on you, and to win you there is not a precious stone I would leave unturned. Conceive a *parure* all of white stones – diamonds, white sapphires, white topazes, tourmalines. Another, of rubies and amethysts, set in gold filigree. Rings that once were poison-combs on Florentine fingers. Red roses for your hair – every petal a hollowed ruby. Amulets and apebuckles, zones and fillets. Aye! know that you would be weeping for wonder before you had seen a tithe of these gauds. Know, too, Miss Dobson, that in the Peerage of France I am Duc d'Etretat et de la Roche Guillaume. Louis Napoleon gave the title to my father for not cutting him in the Bois. I have a house in the Champs Elysées. There is a Swiss in its courtyard. He stands six-foot-seven in his stockings, and the chasseurs are hardly less tall than he. Wherever I go, there are two chefs in my retinue. Both are masters in their art, and furiously jealous of each other. When I compliment either of them on some dish, the other challenges him. They fight with rapiers, next morning, in the garden of whatever house I am occupying. I do not know whether you are greedy? If so, it may interest you to learn that I have a third chef, who makes only soufflés, and an Italian pastry-cook; to say nothing of a Spaniard for salads, an English-woman for roasts, and an Abyssinian for coffee. You found no trace of their handiwork in the meal you have just had with me? No; for in Oxford it is a whim of mine – I may say a point of honour – to lead the ordinary life of an undergraduate. What I eat in this room is cooked by the heavy and unaided hand of Mrs Batch, my landlady. It is set before me by the unaided and – or are you in error? – loving hand of her daughter. Other ministers have I none here. I dispense with my private secretaries. I am unattended by a single valet. So simple a way of life repels you? You would never be called upon to share it. If you married me, I should take my name off the books of my College. I propose that we should spend our honeymoon at Baiae. I have a villa at Baiae. It is there that I keep my grandfather's collection of majolica. The sun shines there always. A long olive-grove secretes the garden from the sea. When you walk in the garden, you know the sea only in blue glimpses through the vacillating leaves. White-gleaming from the bosky shade of this grove are several goddesses. Do you care for Canova? I don't myself. If you do, these figures will appeal to you: they are in his best manner. Do you love the sea? This is not the only house of mine that looks out on it. On the coast of County Clare – am I not Earl of Enniskerry and Baron Shandrin in the Peerage of Ireland? – I have an ancient castle. Sheer from a rock stands it, and the sea has always raged up against its walls. Many ships lie wrecked under that loud implacable sea. But mine is a brave strong castle. No storm affrights it; and not the centuries, clustering houris, with their caresses can seduce it from its hard austerity. I have several titles which for the moment escape me. Baron Llffthwchl am I, and . . . and . . . but you can find them for yourself in Debrett. In me you behold a Prince of the Holy Roman Empire, and a Knight of the Most Noble Order of the Garter. Look well at me! I am Hereditary Comber of the Queen's Lap-Dogs. I am young. I am handsome.

Worldly Considerations

My temper is sweet, and my character without blemish. In fine, Miss Dobson, I am a most desirable *parti*.'

'But,' said Zuleika, 'I don't love you.'

The Duke stamped his foot. 'I beg your pardon,' he said hastily. 'I ought not to have done that. But – you seem to have entirely missed the point of what I was saying.'

'No, I haven't,' said Zuleika.

'Then what,' cried the Duke, standing over her, 'what is your reply?'

Said Zuleika, looking up at him, 'My reply is that I think you are an awful snob.'

Max Beerbohm: Zuleika Dobson

Becky loses her baronet

The news of Lady Crawley's death provoked no more grief or comment than might have been expected in Miss Crawley's family circle. 'I suppose I must put off my party for the 3rd,' Miss Crawley said; and added, after a pause, 'I hope my brother will have the decency not to marry again.' 'What a confounded rage Pitt will be in if he does,' Rawdon remarked, with his usual regard for his elder brother. Rebecca said nothing. She seemed by far the gravest and most impressed of the family. She left the room before Rawdon went away that day; but they met by chance below, as he was going away after taking leave, and had a parley together.

On the morrow, as Rebecca was gazing from the window, she startled Miss Crawley, who was placidly occupied with a French novel, by crying out in an alarmed tone, 'Here's Sir Pitt, Ma'am!' and the Baronet's knock followed this announcement.

'My dear, I can't see him. I won't see him. Tell Bowls not at home, or go downstairs and say I'm too ill to receive any one. My nerves really won't bear my brother at this moment;' cried out Miss Crawley, and resumed her novel.

'She's too ill to see you, sir,' Rebecca said, tripping down to Sir Pitt, who was preparing to ascend.

'So much the better,' Sir Pitt answered. 'I want to see *you*, Miss Becky. Come along a me into the parlour,' and they entered that apartment together.

'I wawnt you back at Queen's Crawley, Miss,' the baronet said, fixing his eyes upon her, and taking off his black gloves and his hat with its great crape hat-band. His eyes had such a strange look, and fixed upon her so steadfastly, that Rebecca Sharp began almost to tremble.

'I hope to come soon,' she said in a low voice, 'as soon as Miss Crawley is better – and return to – to the dear children.'

'You've said to these three months, Becky,' replied Sir Pitt, 'and still you go hanging on to my sister, who'll fling you off like an old shoe, when she's wore you out. I tell you I *want* you. I'm going back to the Vuneral. Will you come back? Yes or no?'

'I daren't – I don't think – it would be right – to be alone – with you, sir,' Becky said, seemingly in great agitation.

'I say agin, I want you,' Sir Pitt said, thumping the table. 'I can't git on without you. I didn't see what it was till you went away. The house all goes wrong. It's not the same place. All my accounts has got muddled agin. You *must* come back. Do come back. Dear Becky, do come.'

'Come – as what, sir?' Rebecca gasped out.

'Come as Lady Crawley, if you like,' the Baronet said, grasping his crape hat. 'There! will that zatusfy you? Come back and be my wife. Your vit vor't. Birth be hanged. You're as good a lady as ever I see. You've got more brains in your little vinger than any baronet's wife in the county. Will you come? Yes or no?'

'Oh, Sir Pitt!' Rebecca said, very much moved.

'Say yes, Becky,' Sir Pitt continued. 'I'm an old man, but a good'n. I'm good for twenty years. I'll make you happy, zee if I don't. You shall do what you like; spend what you like; and 'av it all your own way. I'll make you a zettlement. I'll do everything reglar. Look year!' and the old man fell down on his knees and leered at her like a satyr.

Rebecca started back a picture of consternation. In the course of this history we have never seen her lose her presence of mind; but she did now, and wept some of the most genuine tears that ever fell from her eyes.

'Oh, Sir Pitt!' she said. 'Oh, sir – I – I'm *married already*.'

William Makepeace Thackeray: *Vanity Fair*

Madame Goesler's generosity

Yes; – Madame Goesler was at home. The door was opened by Madame Goesler's own maid, who, smiling, explained that the other servants were all at church. Phineas had become sufficiently intimate at the cottage in Park Lane to be on friendly terms with Madame Goesler's own maid, and now made some little half-familiar remark as to the propriety of his visit during church time. 'Madame will not refuse to see you, I am thinking,' said the girl, who was a German. 'And she is alone?' asked Phineas. 'Alone? Yes; – of course she is alone. Who should be with her now?' Then she took him up into the drawing-room; but, when there, he found that Madame Goesler was absent. 'She shall be down directly,' said the girl. 'I shall tell her who is here, and she will come.'

It was a very pretty room. It may almost be said that there could be no prettier room in all London. It looked out across certain small private gardens, – which were as bright and gay as money could make them when brought into competition with London smoke, – right on to the park. Outside and inside the window, flowers and green things were so arranged that the room itself almost looked as though it were a bower in a garden. And everything in that bower was rich and rare; and there was nothing there which annoyed by its rarity or was distasteful by its richness. The seats, though they were costly as money could buy, were meant for sitting, and were comfortable as seats. There were books for reading, and the means of reading them. Two or three gems of English art were hung upon the walls, and could be seen backwards and forwards in the mirrors.

And there were precious toys lying here and there about the room, – toys very precious, but placed there not because of their price, but because of their beauty. Phineas already knew enough of the art of living to be aware that the woman who had made that room what it was, had charms to add a beauty to everything she touched. What would such a life as his want, if graced by such a companion, – such a life as his might be, if the means which were hers were at his command? It would want one thing, he thought, – the self-respect which he would lose if he were false to the girl who was trusting him with such sweet trust at home in Ireland.

In a very few minutes Madame Goesler was with him, and, though he did not think about it, he perceived that she was bright in her apparel, that her hair was as soft as care could make it, and that every charm belonging to her had been brought into use for his gratification. He almost told himself that he was there in order that he might ask to have all those charms bestowed upon himself. He did not know who had lately come to Park Lane and been a suppliant for the possession of those rich endowments; but I wonder whether they would have been more precious in his eyes had he known that they had so moved the heart of the great Duke as to have induced him to lay his coronet at the lady's feet. I think that had he known that the lady had refused the coronet, that knowledge would have enhanced the value of the prize.

'I am so sorry to have kept you waiting,' she said, as she gave him her hand. 'I was an owl not to be ready for you when you told me that you would come.'

'No; – but a bird of paradise to come to me so sweetly, and at an hour when all the other birds refuse to show the feather of a single wing.'

'And you, – you feel like a naughty boy, do you not, in thus coming out on a Sunday morning?'

'Do you feel like a naughty girl?'

'Yes; – just a little so. I do not know that I should care for everybody to hear that I receive visitors, – or worse still, a visitor, – at this hour on this day. But then it is so pleasant to feel oneself to be naughty! There is a Bohemian flavour of picnic about it which, though it does not come up to the rich gusto of real wickedness, makes one fancy that one is on the border of that delightful region in which there is none of the constraint of custom, – where men and women say what they like, and do what they like.'

'It is pleasant enough to be on the borders,' said Phineas.

'That is just it. Of course decency, morality, and propriety, all made to suit the eye of the public, are the things which are really delightful. We all know that, and live accordingly, – as well as we can. I do at least.'

'And do not I, Madame Goesler?'

'I know nothing about that, Mr Finn, and want to ask no questions. But if you do, I am sure you agree with me that you often envy the improper people, – the Bohemians, – the people who don't trouble themselves about keeping any laws except those for breaking which they would be put into nasty, unpleasant prisons. I envy them. Oh, how I envy them!'

'But you are free as air.'

'The most cabined, cribbed, and confined creature in the world! I have been fighting my way up for the last four years, and have not allowed myself the liberty of one flirtation; – not often even the recreation of a natural laugh. And now I shouldn't wonder if I don't find myself falling back a year or two, just because I have allowed you to come and see me on a Sunday morning. When I told Lotta that you were coming, she shook her head at me in dismay. But now that you are here, tell me what you have done.'

'Nothing as yet, Madame Goesler.'

'I thought it was to have been settled on Friday?'

'It was settled, – before Friday. Indeed, as I look back at it all now, I can hardly tell when it was not settled. It is impossible, and has been impossible, that I should do otherwise. I still hold my place, Madame Goesler, but I have declared that I shall give it up before the debate comes on.'

'It is quite fixed?'

'Quite fixed, my friend.'

'And what next?' Madame Goesler, as she thus interrogated him, was leaning across towards him from the sofa on which she was placed, with both her elbows resting on a small table before her. We all know that look of true interest which the countenance of a real friend will bear when the welfare of his friend is in question. There are doubtless some who can assume it without feeling, – as there are

Worldly Considerations

actors who can personate all the passions. But in ordinary life we think that we can trust such a face, and that we know the true look when we see it. Phineas, as he gazed into Madame Goesler's eyes, was sure that the lady opposite to him was not acting. She at least was anxious for his welfare, and was making his cares her own.

'What next?' said she, repeating her words in a tone that was somewhat hurried.

'I do not know that there will be any next. As far as public life is concerned, there will be no next for me, Madame Goesler.'

'That is out of the question,' she said. 'You are made for public life.'

'Then I shall be untrue to my making, I fear. But to speak plainly –'

'Yes; speak plainly. I want to understand the reality.'

'The reality is this. I shall keep my seat to the end of the session, as I think I may be of use. After that I shall give it up.'

'Resign that too?' she said in a tone of chagrin.

'The chances are, I think, that there will be another dissolution. If they hold their own against Mr Monk's motion, then they will pass an Irish Reform Bill. After that I think they must dissolve.'

'And you will not come forward again?'

'I cannot afford it.'

'Psha! Some five hundred pounds or so!'

'And, besides that, I am well aware that my only chance at my old profession is to give up all idea of Parliament. The two things are not compatible for a beginner at the law. I know it now, and have bought my knowledge by a bitter experience.'

'And where will you live?'

'In Dublin, probably.'

'And you will do, – will do what?'

'Anything honest in a barrister's way that may be brought to me. I hope that I may never descend below that.'

'You will stand up for all the blackguards, and try to make out that the thieves did not steal?'

'It may be that that sort of work may come in my way.'

'And you will wear a wig and try to look wise?'

'The wig is not universal in Ireland, Madame Goesler.'

Worldly Considerations

'And you will wrangle, as though your very soul were in it, for somebody's twenty pounds?'

'Exactly.'

'You have already made a name in the greatest senate in the world, and have governed other countries larger than your own –'

'No; – I have not done that. I have governed no country.'

'I tell you, my friend, that you cannot do it. It is out of the question. Men may move forward from little work to big work; but they cannot move back and do little work, when they have had tasks which were really great. I tell you, Mr Finn, that the House of Parliament is the place for you to work in. It is the only place; – that and the abodes of ministers. Am not I your friend who tell you this?'

'I know that you are my friend.'

'And will you not credit me when I tell you this? What do you fear, that you should run away? You have no wife; – no children. What is the coming misfortune that you dread?' She paused a moment as though for an answer, and he felt that now had come the time in which it would be well that he should tell her of his engagement with his own Mary. She had received him very playfully; but now within the last few minutes there had come upon her a seriousness of gesture, and almost a solemnity of tone, which made him conscious that he should in no way trifle with her. She was so earnest in her friendship that he owed it to her to tell her everything. But before he could think of the words in which his tale should be told, she had gone on with her quick questions. 'Is it solely about money that you fear?' she said.

'It is simply that I have no income on which to live.'

'Have I not offered you money?'

'But, Madame Goesler, you who offer it would yourself despise me if I took it.'

'No; – I do deny it.' As she said this, – not loudly, but with much emphasis, – she came and stood before him where he was sitting. And as he looked at her he could perceive that there was a strength about her of which he had not been aware. She was stronger, larger, more robust physically than he had hitherto conceived. 'I do deny it,' she said. 'Money is neither god nor devil, that it should make one noble and another vile. It is an accident, and, if honestly possessed, may pass from you to me, or from me to you, without a stain. You may take my dinner from me if I give it you, my flowers, my friendship, my, – my, – my everything, but my money! Explain to me the cause of the phenomenon. If I give to you a thousand pounds, now this moment, and you take it, you are base; – but if I leave it you in my will, – and die, – you take it, and are not base. Explain to me the cause of that.'

'You have not said it quite all,' said Phineas hoarsely.

'What have I left unsaid? If I have left anything unsaid, do you say the rest.'

'It is because you are a woman, and young, and beautiful, that no man may take wealth from your hands.'

'Oh, it is that!'

'It is that partly.'

'If I were a man you might take it, though I were young and beautiful as the morning?'

'No; – presents of money are always bad. They stain and load the spirit, and break the heart.'

'And specially when given by a woman's hand?'

'It seems so to me. But I cannot argue of it. Do not let us talk of it any more.'

'Nor can I argue. I cannot argue, but I can be generous, – very generous. I can deny myself for my friend, – can even lower myself in my own esteem for my friend. I can do more than a man can do for a friend. You will not take money from my hand?'

'No, Madame Goesler; – I cannot do that.'

'Take the hand then first. When it and all that it holds are your own, you can help yourself as you list.' So saying, she stood before him with her right hand stretched out towards him.

What man will say that he would not have been tempted? Or what woman will declare that such temptation should have had no force? The very air of the room in which she dwelt was sweet in his nostrils, and there hovered around her an halo of grace and beauty which greeted all his senses. She invited him to join his lot to hers, in order that she might give to him all that was needed to make his life rich and glorious. How would the Ratlers and the Bonteens envy him when they heard of the prize which had become his! The Cantrips and the Greshams would feel that he was a friend doubly valuable, if he could be won back; and Mr Monk would greet him as a fitting ally, – an ally strong with the strength which he had before wanted. With whom would he not be equal? Whom need he fear? Who would not praise him? The story of his poor Mary would be known only in a small village, out beyond the Channel. The temptation certainly was very strong.

But he had not a moment in which to doubt. She was standing there with her face turned from him, but with her hand still stretched towards him. Of course he took it. What man so placed could do other than take a woman's hand?

'My friend,' he said.

'I will be called friend by you no more,' she said. 'You must call me Marie, your own Marie, or you must never call me by any name again. Which shall it be, sir?' He paused a moment, holding her hand, and she let it lie there for an instant while she listened. But still she did not look at him. 'Speak to me! Tell me! Which shall it be?' Still he paused. 'Speak to me. Tell me!' she said again.

'It cannot be as you have hinted to me,' he said at last. His words did not come louder than a low whisper; but they were plainly heard, and instantly the hand was withdrawn.

'Cannot be!' she exclaimed. 'Then I have betrayed myself.'

'No; – Madame Goesler.'

'Sir; I say yes! If you will allow me I will leave you. You will, I know, excuse me if I am abrupt to you.' Then she strode out of the room, and was no more seen of the eyes of Phineas Finn.

Anthony Trollope: Phineas Finn

A question of the dowry

February, 1477
Right worshipful and well-beloved Valentine, in my most humble wise I recommend me unto you. And heartily I thank you for the letter which that ye send me by John Beckerton, whereby I am informed and know that you be purposed to come to Topcroft in

short time, and without any errand or matter but only to have a conclusion of the matter between my father and you. I would be most glad of any creature in life so that this matter might grow to effect. And there, as ye say, an ye come and find the matter no more towards you than ye did aforetime, ye would no more put my father and my lady my mother to no cost nor business for that cause, a good while after – which causeth mine heart to be full heavy: and if that ye come, and the matter take to none effect, then should I be much more sorry and full of heaviness.

And as for myself I have done and understood in the matter that I can and may as good knoweth: and I let you plainly understand that my father will no more money part withal in that behalf but £100 and one mark which is right far from the accomplishment of your desire.

Wherefore if that ye could be content with that good, and my poor person I would be the merriest maiden on ground. And if ye think not yourself so satisfied, or that ye might have much more good, as I have understood by you afore – good, true, and loving Valentine, that ye take no such labour upon you as to come more for that matter but let it pass and never more be spoken of, as I may be your true lover and bede-woman during my life.

No more unto you at this time but Almighty Jesus preserve you both body and soul.

By your Valentine,
M.B.

Margery Brews to John Paston: *The Paston Letters*

A left and a right

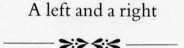

Labouchère was one of the most talented bankers of his generation. It is said that, aged only twenty-two, he asked Hopes if he might be made a partner. He was refused. 'Would it be different if I were Sir Francis Baring's son-in-law?' he asked. 'Yes,' he was told. He then rushed to Francis Baring and asked for the hand of his daughter Dorothy. Baring refused. 'Would it be different if I were a partner in Hope and Co.?' he asked. 'Yes,' he was told. 'Well I am going to be.' He brought off a left and a right, winning both partner and wife.

> Philip Ziegler: *The Sixth Great Power,*
> *Barings 1762–1929*

Love at First Sight

Slava's courtship

I flew to Prague with another singer from the Bolshoi, Alexander Ognivtsev. His bass voice was unique for its power and beauty, and he was handsome; young, tall, broad-shouldered – a regular Russian epic hero. He looked like Chaliapin. From the beginning our friendship was especially close and it always remained so.

We were driven to the Alkron Hotel, and taken to the restaurant for breakfast. All the other visiting Soviet artists were already there. I went in looking for a free table for Sasha [Alexander] and me when I spotted that cellist whose name I couldn't pronounce. He was heading right for me.

'Hello, how good to see you! There's an empty chair at our table – please sit down with us.' He had known that I would be flying in, and had kept that place especially for me. I had scarcely managed to look around when I found myself sitting next to him at his table.

'But I don't know. Where is Sasha going to sit?'

'He'll sit at another table.'

My bearlike friend appeared. 'Where have you been? I've been looking for you. Isn't there a place here for me?'

But Rostropovich told him matter-of-factly, 'You can sit at that table over there.'

As we sat and talked, his thoughts and ideas came pouring down on me like hail. It was only then that I got a good look at him. He was extremely thin, wore glasses, and had a typical intellectual's face. He was young, though already balding, and had an elegant look about him. I later found out that when he learned that I would be in Prague, he brought all his jackets and ties and changed them morning and night, hoping to make an impression.

He was all movement, impulsive, bubbling with jokes; but his eyes, in contrast to his mannerisms, were steady and attentive. It was as if there were two persons within: one trying his best to please, the other observant and shy.

I turned to him. 'Mst . . . Mtl . . . Pardon me, but it's hard to pronounce your name.'

'Just call me Slava. And may I call you Galya?'

'Well, all right.' I wasn't used to being addressed that way; for many years people had been calling me only Galina Pavlovna. All my male acquaintances regarded me as, above all, a famous singer, and our relationships amounted to flowers and compliments; they all perceived me as the person they had seen on stage and whom they had applauded. And they were all middle-aged. Also, I had a reliable husband much older than myself, and that left a certain imprint on my behavior. This Slava was treating me like a girl!

And he saw me as such. He had never seen me on stage – for him I was not a spoiled, capricious prima donna but simply a young woman. With all his directness and impetuosity, he began to court me. Neither my past nor my rising fame interested him. It was a strange experience for me, but the impression it produced was special: his was a naturalness and sincerity that I was unaccustomed to.

When we went out to the street near the hotel, we saw a woman with a basket full of lilies of the valley. He took the whole armful and gave it to me.

Rehearsals, performances . . . and at my side would appear, then disappear, a man with a kind of frantic motor inside him. I didn't have time to analyse my own feelings and motives, but there I was looking forward to our meetings.

He came into my hotel room, sat down at the piano, and played. 'Too bad I have a concert and won't be able to hear you in *Onegin* tonight. You must be a marvelous Tatyana.'

Suddenly he leapt from the piano and sank to his knees. I was startled. Should I turn the whole thing into a joke?

'Forgive me, but in Moscow, the first time we met, I noticed that you had very beautiful legs – I wanted to kiss your feet then. You have to be at the theatre soon, so I'll go. Till tomorrow!'

My head was in a muddle. At the theatre there were flowers from him. Although I was often pampered, his attention was unlike any other I had ever known. Or perhaps I was now different?

Love at First Sight

Sasha sang the role of Gremin in our *Onegin*. After the performance he asked me, 'Why do I see you so seldom? Let's go for a walk tomorrow.'

'Fine, five o'clock.'

Slava later confessed that Sasha had asked to be awakened at five. And he had told Slava about our walk. At four-thirty, Slava showed up at my door. 'Let's go for a walk. The weather is marvellous. Have you been to the park on the hill?'

'But I promised Sasha I'd go with him. He'll be offended.'

'Your Sasha is sleeping like a bear in the dead of winter. If he isn't awakened, he'll sleep right through until morning.'

'Nonsense.'

'Here's how we'll settle it: We'll knock on his door three times. If he doesn't wake up, we'll call it fate, and you can come with me.'

We went to Sasha's door and Slava knocked three times. Of course he could have knocked more loudly, but I didn't insist. No answer. Slava took me by the hand, and we ran out to the street.

Never before had I felt so free and natural with someone. He talked about his mother and sister as if he and I had known each other for a long time. And how young he was! Although we were the same age, it seemed to me that he was a mere boy.

We left the path and walked into a deep thicket. Ahead of us was a high stone fence. 'Slava, we have to go back and look for the road.'

'Why go back? We'll climb over the fence.'

'What do you mean, "climb over the fence"? I can't . . .'

'Why not? I'll give you a boost so you can get up on top of the fence. Then I'll climb over it and catch you from the other side.'

That was the last straw. But what could I do? I climbed up, trying not to lose my composure. He was already on the other side, shouting at me, 'Jump!'

'Where to? Look, there are puddles and mud everywhere!'

'You're right, I hadn't noticed. But never mind. Here.' And he threw his coat over a puddle.

It was getting close to dinner time and we had to go back. We hurried along the street. 'Look, Slava, pickles! Too bad the store is closed.'

'Do you like pickles?'

'I adore them!'

In the hotel we sat down at the table as if we had just met up with each other in the lobby. God forbid that the others should notice anything! I was well-lodged in the first stages of a love affair, and on my first trip at that! It would have been considered a disgrace to the moral standing of the Soviet People. If anyone found out, I would never be allowed to go abroad again.

My 'bodyguard,' Sasha, came into the restaurant like a bear coming out of its den. He really did look sleepy. 'Where have you been? I've been looking for you everywhere. And you! Why didn't you wake me up?'

'But I knocked! We both knocked! We almost broke the door down. You sure can sleep!'

Then Slava began to tell stories. Jokes flowed from him as from a cornucopia. Never in my life did I laugh so much as I did that evening. Then, quite abruptly, he jumped up and ran off. What an odd sort of man! Within, he seemed to be all perpetual motion.

I came back to my room and threw open my closet to get my night clothes. The sight behind the door made me leap back in fear. In the closet, like a white spectre, stood a huge crystal vase overflowing with lilies of the valley and pickles. Now, when had he found time to do that?

I called him in his room. 'Why did you do that?'

'Did you like it? I'm glad. Good night.'

We were hurtling toward one another, and no force on earth could stop us. As a woman of twenty-eight who had been taught much by experience, I wholeheartedly felt his young, unrestrained passion. And all my feelings, which for so long had been pent up within, went out to him in response.

We had only been in golden Prague for four days, but we were already in fact man and wife, although no one else knew about it. We decided that when we got back to Moscow we would get married.

Neither of us had ever heard the other perform. And to be honest, a cellist to me was some nameless individual in the orchestra pit. But my future husband had told me with some pride that he was also an assistant professor at the Moscow Conservatory.

At the end of those four days in Prague I got a telegram from the Ministry of Culture telling me to prepare for a trip to Yugoslavia right away. A government delegation – Bulganin, Khrushchev, Mikoyan, and others – was going to Belgrade, and would be accompanied by a group of artists. I wasn't asked whether I wanted to go – I was merely told to pack my things and get into a car.

Slava would be in Prague for another week. He flew from store to store, buying dishes, chandeliers, blankets . . . He saw himself as the future head of a happy family. With an intensity typical of him, he decided that when I got back to Moscow I should go directly from the airport to his place, without stopping at home.

'But how can I part in that way from a man I've lived with for ten years? He never did me any harm.'

'Then tell him everything, get it over with, and call me when you're through. I'll be waiting for you.'

Galina Vishnevskaya: *Galina*;
translated by Guy Daniels

Heart struck

A new operette, *The Fair Captive of Samarcand*, was being enacted, and the frequenters of Garble's were all curious to behold the *débutante*, Jenny Mere, who was said to be both pretty and talented. These predictions were surely fulfilled, when the captive peeped from the window of her wooden turret. She looked so pale under her blue turban. Her eyes were dark with fear; her parted lips did not seem capable of speech. 'Is it that she is frightened of us?' the audience wondered. 'Or of the flashing scimitar of Aphoschaz, the cruel father who holds her captive?' So they gave her loud applause, and when at length she jumped down, to be caught in the arms of her gallant lover, Nissarah, and, throwing aside her Eastern draperies, did a simple dance in the convention of Columbine, their delight was quite unbounded. She was very young and did not dance very well, it is true, but they forgave her that. And when she turned in the dance and saw her father with his scimitar, their hearts beat swiftly for her. Nor were all eyes tearless when she pleaded with him for her life.

Strangely absorbed, quite callous of his two companions, Lord George gazed over the footlights. He seemed as one who is in a trance. Of a sudden, something shot sharp into his heart. In pain he sprang to his feet and, as he turned, he seemed to see a winged and laughing child, in whose hand was a bow, fly swiftly away into the darkness. At his side, was the Dwarf's chair. It was empty. Only La Gambogi was with him, and her dark face was like the face of a fury.

Presently he sank back into his chair, holding one hand to his heart, that still throbbed from the strange transfixion. He breathed very painfully and seemed scarce conscious of his surroundings. But La Gambogi knew he would pay no more homage to her now, for that the love of Jenny Mere had come into his heart.

When the operette was over, his lovesick Lordship snatched up his cloak and went away without one word to the lady at his side. Rudely he brushed aside Count Karoloff and Mr FitzClarence, with whom he had arranged to play hazard. Of his comrades, his cynicism, his reckless scorn – of all the material of his existence – he was oblivious now. He had no time for penitence or diffident delay. He only knew that he must kneel at the feet of Jenny Mere and ask her to be his wife.

'Miss Mere,' said Garble, 'is in her room, resuming her ordinary attire. If your Lordship deign to await the conclusion of her humble toilet, it shall be my privilege to present her to your Lordship. Even now, indeed, I hear her footfall on the stair.'

Lord George uncovered his head and with one hand nervously smoothed his rebellious wig.

'Miss Mere, come hither,' said Garble. 'This is my Lord George Hell, that you have pleased whom by your poor efforts this night will ever be the prime gratification of your passage through the roseate realms of art.'

Little Miss Mere, who had never seen a lord, except in fancy or in dreams, curtseyed shyly and hung her head. With a loud crash, Lord George fell on his knees. The manager was greatly surprised, the girl greatly embarrassed. Yet neither of them laughed, for sincerity dignified his posture and sent eloquence from its lips.

'Miss Mere,' he cried, 'give ear, I pray you, to my poor words, nor spurn me in misprision from the pedestal of your Beauty, Genius, and Virtue. All too conscious, alas! of my presumption in the same, I yet abase myself before you as a suitor for your adorable Hand. I grope under the shadow of your raven Locks. I am dazzled in the light of those translucent Orbs, your Eyes. In the intolerable Whirlwind of your Fame I faint and am afraid.'

'Sir –' the girl began, simply.

'Say "My Lord,"' said Garble, solemnly.

'My Lord, I thank you for your words. They are beautiful. But indeed, indeed, I can never be your bride.'

Lord George hid his face in his hands.

'Child,' said Mr Garble, 'let not the sun rise ere you have retracted those wicked words.'

'My wealth, my rank, my irremeable love for you, I throw them at your feet,' Lord George cried piteously. 'I would wait an hour, a week, a lustre, even a decade, did you but bid me hope!'

'I can never be your wife,' she said, slowly. 'I can never be the wife of any man whose face is not saintly. Your face, my Lord, mirrors, it may be, true love for me, but it is even as a mirror long tarnished by the reflexion of this world's vanity. It is even as a tarnished mirror. Do not kneel to me, for I am poor and humble. I was not made for such impetuous wooing. Kneel, if you please, to some greater, gayer lady. As for my love, it is my own, nor can it be ever torn from me, but given, as true love must needs be given, freely. Ah, rise from your knees. That man, whose face is wonderful as are the faces of the saints, to him I will give my true love.'

Miss Mere, though visibly affected, had spoken this speech with a gesture and elocution so superb, that Mr Garble could not help applauding, deeply though he regretted her attitude towards his honoured patron. As for Lord George, he was immobile as a stricken oak. With a sweet look of pity, Miss Mere went her way, and Mr Garble, with some solicitude, helped his Lordship to rise from his knees. Out into the night, without a word, his Lordship went. Above him the stars were still splendid. They seemed to mock the festoons of little lamps, dim now and guttering, in the garden of Garble's. What should he do? No thoughts came; only his heart burnt hotly. He stood on the brim of Garble's lake, shallow and artificial as his past life had been. Two swans slept on its surface.

Love at First Sight

The moon shone strangely upon their white, twisted necks. Should he drown himself? There was no one in the garden to prevent him, and in the morning they would find him floating there, one of the noblest of love's victims. The garden would be closed in the evening. There would be no performance in the little theatre. It might be that Jenny Mere would mourn him. 'Life is a prison, without bars,' he murmured, as he walked away.

Max Beerbohm: *The Happy Hypocrite*

Oroonoko and Imoinda

Oroonoko coming from the wars (which were now ended) after he had made his court to his grandfather, he thought in honour he ought to make a visit to Imoinda, the daughter of his foster-father, the dead General; and to make some excuse to her, because his preservation was the occasion of her father's death; and to present her with those slaves that had been taken in this last battle, as the trophies of her father's victories. When he came, attended by all the young soldiers of any merit, he was infinitely surpris'd at the beauty of this fair queen of night, whose face and person was so exceeding all he had ever beheld, that lovely modesty with which she receiv'd him, that softness in her look and sighs, upon the melancholy occasion of this honour that was done by so great a man as Oroonoko, and a Prince of whom she had heard such admirable things; the awfulness wherewith she receiv'd him, and the sweetness of her words and behaviour while he stay'd, gain'd a perfect conquest over his fierce heart, and made him feel, the victor cou'd be subdu'd. So that having made his first compliments, and presented her an hundred and fifty slaves in fetters, he told her with his eyes, that he was not insensible of her charms; while Imoinda, who wished for nothing more than so glorious a conquest, was pleas'd to believe, she understood that silent language of new-born love; and, from that moment, put on all her additions to beauty.

Love at First Sight

The Prince return'd to Court with quite another humour than before; and though he did not speak much of the fair Imoinda, he had the pleasure to hear all his followers speak of nothing but the charms of that maid, insomuch that, even in the presence of the old King, they were extolling her, and heightning, if possible, the beauties they had found in her: so that nothing else was talk'd of, no other sound was heard in every corner where there were whisperers, but Imoinda! Imoinda!

'Twill be imagined Oroonoko stay'd not long before he made his second visit; nor, considering his quality, not much longer before he told her, he ador'd her. I have often heard him say, that he admir'd by what strange inspiration he came to talk things so soft, and so passionate, who never knew love, nor was us'd to the conversation of women; but (to use his own words) he said, most happily, some new, and, till then, unknown power instructed his heart and tongue in the language of love, and at the same time, in favour of him, inspir'd Imoinda with a sense of his passion. She was touch'd with what he said, and return'd it all in such answers as went to his very heart, with a pleasure unknown before. Nor did he use those obligations ill, that love had done him, but turn'd all his happy moments to the best advantage; and as he knew no vice, his flame aim'd at nothing but honour, if such a distinction may be made in love; and especially in that country, where men take to themselves as many as they can maintain; and where the only crime and sin with woman, is, to turn her off, to abandon her to want, shame and misery: such ill morals are only practis'd in Christian countries, where they prefer the bare name of religion; and, without virtue or morality, think that sufficient. But Oroonoko was none of those professors; but as he had right notions of honour, so he made her such propositions as were not only and barely such; but, contrary to the custom of his country, he made her vows, she shou'd be the only woman he wou'd possess while he liv'd; that no age or wrinkles shou'd encline him to change; for her soul wou'd be always fine, and always young; and he shou'd have an eternal idea in his mind of the charms she now bore; and shou'd look into his heart for that idea, when he cou'd find it no longer in her face.

After a thousand assurances of his lasting flame, and her eternal empire over him, she condescended to receive him for her husband;

or rather, receiv'd him, as the greatest honour the gods cou'd do her.

Aphra Behn: *Oroonoko*

A look before leaping

In his Utopia (Sir Thomas More's) his lawe is that the young people are to see each other stark naked before marriage.

Sir William Roper, of Eltham, in Kent, came one morning pretty early, to my lord, with a proposall to marry one of his daughters. My lord's daughters were then both together abed in a truckle-bed in their father's chamber asleep. He carries Sir William into the chamber and takes the sheete by the corner and suddenly whippes it off. They lay on their Backs and their Smocks up as high as their armpitts. This awakened them, and immediately they turned on their Bellies. Quoth Roper, 'I have seen both sides,' and so gave a patt on her Buttock, he made choice (of Margaret) sayeing, 'Thou art mine.'

John Aubrey: *Brief Lives*

Unwelcome Approaches

Blood bond

. . . Deeming it expedient to soothe him, she took one of his hands in hers, placed the other hand on his shoulder, looked up in his face with a winning seriousness and said in the tenderest possible tone,

'What would you have, Scythrop?'

Scythrop was in heaven again. 'What would I have? What but you, Marionetta? You for the companion of my studies, the partner of my thoughts, the auxiliary of my great designs for the emancipation of mankind.'

'I am afraid I should be but a poor auxiliary, Scythrop. What would you have me do?'

'Do as Rosalia does with Carlos, divine Marionetta. Let us each open a vein in the other's arm, mix our blood in a bowl, and drink it as a sacrament of love. Then we shall see visions of transcendental illumination, and soar on the wings of ideas into the space of pure intelligence.'

Marionetta could not reply; she had not so strong a stomach as Rosalia, and turned sick at the proposition. She disengaged herself suddenly from Scythrop, sprang through the door of the tower and fled with precipitation along the corridors.

Thomas Love Peacock: *Nightmare Abbey*

Filing a declaration

Mr Guppy sat down at the table, and began nervously sharpening the carving-knife on the carving-fork; still looking at me (as I felt quite sure without looking at him), in the same unusual manner. The sharpening lasted so long, that at last I felt a kind of obligation on me to raise my eyes, in order that I might break the spell under which he seemed to labour, of not being able to leave off.

He immediately looked at the dish, and began to carve.

'What will you take yourself, miss? You'll take a morsel of something?'

'No, thank you,' said I.

'Shan't I give you a piece of anything at all, miss?' said Mr Guppy, hurriedly drinking off a glass of wine.

'Nothing, thank you,' said I. 'I have only waited to see that you have everything you want. Is there anything I can order for you?'

'No, I am much obliged to you, miss, I'm sure. I've everything that I can require to make me comfortable – at least I – not comfortable – I'm never that:' he drank off two more glasses of wine, one after another.

I thought I had better go.

'I beg your pardon, miss!' said Mr Guppy, rising, when he saw me rise. 'But would you allow me the favour of a minute's private conversation?'

Not knowing what to say, I sat down again.

'What follows is without prejudice, miss?' said Mr Guppy, anxiously bringing a chair towards my table.

'I don't understand what you mean,' said I, wondering.

'It's one of our law terms, miss. You won't make any use of it to my detriment, at Kenge and Carboy's, or elsewhere. If our conversation shouldn't lead to anything, I am to be as I was, and am not to be prejudiced in my situation or worldly prospects. In short, it's in total confidence.'

'I am at a loss, sir,' said I, 'to imagine what you can have to communicate in total confidence to me, whom you have never seen but once; but I should be very sorry to do you any injury.'

'Thank you, miss. I'm sure of it – that's quite sufficient.' All this time Mr Guppy was either planing his forehead with his handkerchief, or tightly rubbing the palm of his left hand with the palm of his right. 'If you would excuse my taking another glass of wine, miss, I think it might assist me in getting on, without a continual choke that cannot fail to be mutually unpleasant.'

He did so, and came back again. I took the opportunity of moving well behind my table.

'You wouldn't allow me to offer you one, would you, miss?' said Mr Guppy, apparently refreshed.

'Not any,' said I.

'Not half a glass?' said Mr Guppy; 'quarter? No! Then, to proceed. My present salary, Miss Summerson, at Kenge and Carboy's, is two pound a week. When I first had the happiness of looking upon you, it was one-fifteen, and had stood at that figure for a lengthened period. A rise of five has since taken place, and a further rise of five is guaranteed at the expiration of a term not exceeding twelve months from the present date. My mother has a little property, which takes the form of a small life annuity; upon which she lives in an independent though unassuming manner, in the Old Street Road. She is eminently calculated for a mother-in-law. She never interferes, is all for peace, and her disposition easy. She has her failings – as who has not? – but I never knew her do it when company was present; at which time you may freely trust her with wines, spirits, or malt liquors. My own abode is lodgings at Penton Place, Pentonville. It is lowly, but airy, open at the back, and considered one of the 'ealthiest outlets. Miss Summerson! In the mildest language, I adore you. Would you be so kind as to allow me (as I may say) to file a declaration – to make an offer!'

Mr Guppy went down on his knees. I was well behind my table, and not much frightened. I said, 'Get up from that ridiculous position immediately, sir, or you will oblige me to break my implied promise and ring the bell!'

Unwelcome Approaches

'Hear me out, miss!' said Mr Guppy, folding his hands.

'I cannot consent to hear another word, sir,' I returned, 'unless you get up from the carpet directly, and go and sit down at the table, as you ought to do if you have any sense at all.'

He looked piteously, but slowly rose and did so.

'Yet what a mockery it is, miss,' he said, with his hand upon his heart, and shaking his head at me in a melancholy manner over the tray, 'to be stationed behind food at such a moment. The soul recoils from food at such a moment, miss.'

'I beg you to conclude,' said I; 'you have asked me to hear you out, and I beg you to conclude.'

'I will, miss,' said Mr Guppy. 'As I love and honour, so likewise I obey. Would that I could make Thee the subject of that vow, before the shrine!'

'That is quite impossible,' said I, 'and entirely out of the question.'

'I am aware,' said Mr Guppy, leaning forward over the tray, and regarding me, as I again strangely felt, though my eyes were not directed to him, with his late intent look, 'I am aware that in a worldly point of view, according to all appearances, my offer is a poor one. But, Miss Summerson! Angel! – No, don't ring – I have been brought up in a sharp school, and am accustomed to a variety of general practice. Though a young man, I have ferreted out evidence, got up cases, and seen lots of life. Blest with your hand, what means might I not find of advancing your interests, and pushing your fortunes! What might I not get to know, nearly concerning you? I know nothing now, certainly; but what *might* I not, if I had your confidence, and you set me on?'

I told him that he addressed my interest, or what he supposed to be my interest, quite as unsuccessfully as he addressed my inclination; and he would now understand that I requested him, if he pleased, to go away immediately.

'Cruel miss,' said Mr Guppy, 'hear but another word! I think you must have seen that I was struck with those charms, on the day when I waited at the Whytorseller. I think you must have remarked that I could not forbear a tribute to those charms when I put up the steps of the 'ackney-coach. It was a feeble tribute to Thee, but it was well meant. Thy image has ever since been fixed in my breast. I

Unwelcome Approaches

have walked up and down, of an evening, opposite Jellyby's house, only to look upon the bricks that once contained Three. This out of to-day, quite an unnecessary out so far as the attendance, which was its pretended object, went, was planned by me alone for Thee alone. If I speak of interest, it is only to recommend myself and my respectful wretchedness. Love was before it, and is before it.'

'I should be pained, Mr Guppy,' said I, rising and putting my hand upon the bell-rope, 'to do you, or any one who was sincere, the injustice of slighting any honest feeling, however disagreeably expressed. If you have really meant to give me a proof of your good opinion, though ill-timed and misplaced, I feel that I ought to thank you. I have very little reason to be proud, and I am not proud. I hope,' I think I added, without very well knowing what I said, 'that you will now go away as if you had never been so exceedingly foolish, and attend to Messrs Kenge and Carboy's business.'

'Half a minute, miss!' cried Mr Guppy, checking me as I was about to ring. 'This has been without prejudice?'

'I will never mention it,' said I, 'unless you should give me future occasion to do so.'

'A quarter of a minute, miss! In case you should think better – at any time, however distant, *that's* no consequence, for my feelings can never alter – of anything I have said, particularly what might I not do – Mr William Guppy, eighty-seven, Penton Place, or if removed, or dead (of blighted hopes or anything of that sort), care of Mrs Guppy, three hundred and two, Old Street Road, will be sufficient.'

I rang the bell, the servant came, and Mr Guppy, laying his written card upon the table, and making a dejected bow, departed. Raising my eyes as he went out, I once more saw him looking at me after he had passed the door.

I sat there for another hour or more, finishing my books and payments, and getting through plenty of business. Then, I arranged my desk, and put everything away, and was so composed and cheerful that I thought I had quite dismissed this unexpected incident. But, when I went up-stairs to my own room, I surprised myself by beginning to laugh about it, and then surprised myself still more by beginning to cry about it. In short, I was in a flutter for a little while; and felt as if an old chord had been more coarsely touched than it ever had been since the days of the dear old doll, long buried in the garden.

Charles Dickens: *Bleak House*

Mr Collins proposes

The next day opened a new scene at Longbourn. Mr Collins made his declaration in form. Having resolved to do it without loss of time, as his leave of absence extended only to the following Saturday, and having no feelings of diffidence to make it distressing to himself even at the moment, he sat about it in a very orderly manner, with all the observances, which he supposed a regular part of the business. On finding Mrs Bennet, Elizabeth, and one of the younger girls together soon after breakfast, he addressed the mother in these words: 'May I hope, madam, for your interest with your fair daughter Elizabeth, when I solicit for the honour of a private audience with her in the course of this morning?'

Before Elizabeth had time for anything but a blush of surprise, Mrs Bennet instantly answered, 'Oh dear! – Yes – certainly. I am sure Lizzy will be very happy – I am sure she can have no objection. Come, Kitty, I want you upstairs.' And, gathering her work together, she was hastening away, when Elizabeth called out,

'Dear madam, do not go. I beg you will not go. Mr Collins must excuse me. He can have nothing to say to me that anybody need not hear. I am going away myself.'

'No, no, nonsense, Lizzy. I desire you will stay where you are.' And upon Elizabeth's seeming really, with vexed and embarrassed looks, about to escape, she added, 'Lizzy, I *insist* upon your staying and hearing Mr Collins.'

Elizabeth would not oppose such an injunction – and a moment's consideration making her also sensible that it would be wisest to get it over as soon and as quietly as possible, she sat down again, and tried to conceal, by incessant employment, the feelings which were divided between distress and diversion. Mrs Bennet and Kitty walked off, and as soon as they were gone Mr Collins began.

'Believe me, my dear Miss Elizabeth, that your modesty, so far from doing you any disservice, rather adds to your other perfections. You would have been less amiable in my eyes had there *not* been this little unwillingness; but allow me to assure you, that I have your respected mother's permission for this address. You can hardly doubt the purport of my discourse, however your natural delicacy may lead you to dissemble; my attentions have been too marked to be mistaken. Almost as soon as I entered the house, I singled you out as the companion of my future life. But before I am run away with by my feelings on this subject, perhaps it would be advisable for me to state my reasons for marrying – and, moreover, for coming into Hertfordshire with the design of selecting a wife, as I certainly did.'

The idea of Mr Collins, with all his solemn composure, being run away with by his feelings, made Elizabeth so near laughing, that she could not use the short pause he allowed in any attempt to stop him farther, and he continued:–

'My reasons for marrying are, first, that I think it a right thing for every clergyman in easy circumstances (like myself) to set the example of matrimony in his parish; secondly, that I am convinced it will add very greatly to my happiness; and thirdly – which perhaps I ought to have mentioned earlier, that it is the particular advice and recommendation of the very noble lady whom I have the honour of calling patroness. Twice has she condescended to give me her opinion (unasked too!) on this subject; and it was but the very Saturday night before I left Hunsford – between our pools at quadrille, while Mrs Jenkinson was arranging Miss de Bourgh's footstool, that she said, 'Mr Collins, you must marry. A clergyman like you must marry. – Chuse properly, chuse a gentlewoman for *my* sake; and for your *own*, let her be an active, useful sort of person, not brought up high, but able to make a small income go a good way. This is my advice. Find such a woman as soon as you can, bring her to Hunsford, and I will visit her.' Allow me, by the way, to observe, my fair cousin, that I do not reckon the notice and kindness of Lady Catherine de Bourgh as among the least of the advantages in my power to offer. You will find her manners beyond anything I can describe; and your wit and vivacity, I think, must be acceptable to her, especially when tempered with the silence and respect which her rank will inevitably excite. Thus much for my general intention in favour of matrimony; it remains to be told why my views were directed to Longbourn instead of my own neighbourhood, where I assure you there are many amiable young women. But the fact is, that being, as I am, to inherit this estate after the death of your honoured father (who, however, may live many years longer), I could not satisfy myself without resolving to chuse a wife from among his daughters, that the loss to them might be as little as possible, when the melancholy event takes place – which, however, as I have already said, may not be for several years. This has been my motive, my fair cousin, and I flatter myself it will not sink me in your esteem. And now nothing remains for me but to assure you in the most animated language of the violence of my affection. To fortune I am perfectly indifferent, and shall make no demand of that nature on your father, since I am well aware that it could not be complied with; and that one thousand pounds in the 4 per cents., which will not be yours till after your mother's decease, is all that you may ever be entitled to. On that head, therefore, I shall be uniformly silent; and you may assure yourself that no ungenerous reproach shall ever pass my lips when we are married.'

It was absolutely necessary to interrupt him now.

'You are too hasty, sir,' she cried. 'You forget that I have made no answer. Let me do it without further loss of time. Accept my thanks for the compliment you are paying me. I am very sensible of the honour of your proposals, but it is impossible for me to do otherwise than decline them.'

'I am not now to learn,' replied Mr Collins, with a formal wave of the hand, 'that it is usual with young ladies to reject the addresses of the man whom they secretly mean to accept, when he first applies for their favour; and that sometimes the refusal is repeated a second or even a third time. I am therefore by no means discouraged by what you have just said, and shall hope to lead you to the altar ere long.'

'Upon my word, sir,' cried Elizabeth, 'your hope is rather an extraordinary one after my declaration. I do assure you that I am not

Unwelcome Approaches

one of those young ladies (if such young ladies there are) who are so daring as to risk their happiness on the chance of being asked a second time. I am perfectly serious in my refusal. You could not make *me* happy, and I am convinced that I am the last woman in the world who would make *you* so. Nay, were your friend Lady Catherine to know me, I am persuaded she would find me in every respect ill qualified for the situation.'

'Were it certain that Lady Catherine would think so,' said Mr Collins very gravely – 'but I cannot imagine that her ladyship would at all disapprove of you. And you may be certain that when I have the honour of seeing her again, I shall speak in the highest terms of your modesty, economy, and other amiable qualifications.'

'Indeed, Mr Collins, all praise of me will be unnecessary. You must give me leave to judge for myself, and pay me the compliment of believing what I say. I wish you very happy and very rich, and by refusing your hand, do all in my power to prevent your being otherwise. In making me the offer, you must have satisfied the delicacy of your feelings with regard to my family, and may take possession of Longbourn estate whenever it falls without any self-reproach. This matter may be considered, therefore, as finally settled.' And rising as she thus spoke, she would have quitted the room, had not Mr Collins thus addressed her:

'When I do myself the honour of speaking to you next on the subject, I shall hope to receive a more favourable answer than you have now given me; though I am far from accusing you of cruelty at present, because I know it to be the established custom of your sex to reject a man on the first application, and perhaps you have even now said as much to encourage my suit as would be consistent with the true delicacy of the female character.'

'Really, Mr Collins,' cried Elizabeth with some warmth, 'you puzzle me exceedingly. If what I have hitherto said can appear to you in the form of encouragement, I know not how to express my refusal in such a way as may convince you of its being one.'

'You must give me leave to flatter myself, my dear cousin, that your refusal of my addresses is merely words of course. My reasons for believing it are briefly these: – It does not appear to me that my hand is unworthy your acceptance, or that the establishment I can

Unwelcome Approaches

offer would be any other than highly desirable. My situation in life, my connections with the family of de Bourgh, and my relationship to your own, are circumstances highly in my favour; and you should take it into further consideration, that in spite of your manifold attractions, it is by no means certain that another offer of marriage may ever be made you. Your portion is unhappily so small, that it will in all likelihood undo the effects of your loveliness and amiable qualifications. As I must therefore conclude that you are not serious in your rejection of me, I shall chuse to attribute it to your wish of increasing my love by suspense, according to the usual practice of elegant females.'

'I do assure you, sir, that I have no pretensions whatever to that kind of elegance which consists in tormenting a respectable man. I would rather be paid the compliment of being believed sincere. I thank you again and again for the honour you have done me in your proposals, but to accept them is absolutely impossible. My feelings in every respect forbid it. Can I speak plainer? Do not consider me now as an elegant female, intending to plague you, but as a rational creature, speaking the truth from her heart.'

'You are uniformly charming!' cried he, with an air of awkward gallantry; 'and I am persuaded that when sanctioned by the express authority of both your excellent parents, my proposals will not fail of being acceptable.'

To such perseverance in wilful self-deception Elizabeth would make no reply, and immediately and in silence withdrew; determined, that if he persisted in considering her repeated refusals as flattering encouragement, to apply to her father, whose negative might be uttered in such a manner as must be decisive, and whose behaviour at least could not be mistaken for the affectation and coquetry of an elegant female.

Jane Austen: *Pride and Prejudice*

High Romance

Under the moon

'Lucy, did you never dream of meeting me?'
'O Richard! yes; for I remembered you.'
'Lucy! and did you pray that we might meet?'
'I did!'

Young as when she looked upon the lovers in Paradise, the fair Immortal journeys onward. Fronting her, it is not night but veiled day. Full half the sky is flushed. Not darkness: not day; but the nuptials of the two.

'My own! my own for ever! You are pledged to me? Whisper!'

He hears the delicious music.

'And you are mine?'

A soft beam travels to the fern-covert under the pine-wood where they sit, and for answer he has her eyes: turned to him an instant, timidly fluttering over the depths of his, and then downcast; for through her eyes her soul is naked to him.

'Lucy! my bride! my life!'

The night-jar spins his dark monotony on the branch of the pine. The soft beam travels round them, and listens to their hearts. Their lips are locked.

Pipe no more, Love, for a time! Pipe as you will you cannot express their first kiss; nothing of its sweetness, and of the sacredness of it, nothing. St Cecilia up aloft, before the silver organ-pipes of Paradise, pressing fingers upon all the notes of which Love is but one, from her you may hear it.

George Meredith: *The Ordeal of Richard Feverel*

Lord Orville declares himself

We all went together to the drawing-room. After a short and unentertaining conversation, Mrs Selwyn said she must prepare for her journey, and begged me to see for some books she had left in the parlour.

And here, while I was looking for them, I was followed by Lord Orville. He shut the door after he came in, and approaching me with a look of anxiety, said, 'Is this true, Miss Anville? are you going?'

'I believe so, my Lord,' said I, still looking for the books.

'So suddenly, so unexpectedly, must I lose you?'

'No great loss, my Lord,' cried I, endeavouring to speak chearfully.

'Is it possible,' said he, gravely, 'Miss Anville can doubt my sincerity?'

'I can't imagine,' cried I, 'what Mrs Selwyn has done with these books.'

'Would to Heaven,' continued he, 'I might flatter myself you would allow me to prove it!'

'I must run up stairs,' cried I, greatly confused, 'and ask what she has done with them.'

'You are going, then,' cried he, taking my hand, 'and you give me not the smallest hope of your return! – will you not, then, my too lovely friend! – will you not, at least, teach me, with fortitude like your own, to support your absence?'

'My Lord,' cried I, endeavouring to disengage my hand, 'pray let me go!'

'I will,' cried he, to my inexpressible confusion, dropping on one knee, 'if you wish to leave me!'

'Oh, my Lord,' exclaimed I, 'rise, I beseech you, rise! – such a posture to me! – surely your Lordship is not so cruel as to mock me!'

'Mock you!' repeated he earnestly; 'no, I revere you! I esteem and I admire you above all human beings! you are the friend to whom my soul is attached as to its better half! you are the most amiable, the most perfect of women! and you are dearer to me than language has the power of telling.'

I attempt not to describe my sensations at that moment; I scarce breathed; I doubted if I existed, – the blood forsook my cheeks, and my feet refused to sustain me: Lord Orville, hastily rising, supported me to a chair, upon which I sunk, almost lifeless.

For a few minutes, we neither of us spoke; and then, seeing me recover, Lord Orville, though in terms hardly articulate, entreated my pardon for his abruptness. The moment my strength returned, I attempted to rise, but he would not permit me.

I cannot write the scene that followed, though every word is engraven on my heart: but his protestations, his expressions, were too flattering for repetition: nor would he, in spite of my repeated efforts to leave him, suffer me to escape; – in short, my dear Sir, I was not proof against his solicitations – and he drew from me the most sacred secret of my heart!

Fanny Burney: Evelina

Linda and Fabrice

All through those terrible months of May, June, and July, Linda waited for a sign from Fabrice, but no sign came. She did not doubt that he was still alive, it was not in Linda's nature to imagine that anyone might be dead. She knew that thousands of Frenchmen were in German hands, but felt certain that, had Fabrice been taken prisoner (a thing which she did not at all approve of, incidentally, taking the old-fashioned view that, unless in exceptional circumstances, it is a disgrace), he would undoubtedly manage to escape.

She would hear from him before long, and, meanwhile, there was nothing to be done, she must simply wait. All the same, as the days went by with no news, and as all the news there was from France was bad, she did become exceedingly restless. She was really more concerned with his attitude than with his safety – his attitude towards events and his attitude towards her. She felt sure that he would never be associated with the armistice, she felt sure that he would want to communicate with her, but she had no proof, and, in moments of great loneliness and depression, she allowed herself to lose faith. She realised how little she really knew of Fabrice, he had seldom talked seriously to her, their relationship having been primarily physical while their conversations and chat had all been based on jokes.

They had laughed and made love and laughed again, and the months had slipped by with no time for anything but laughter and love. Enough to satisfy her, but what about him? Now that life had become so serious, and, for a Frenchman, so tragic, would he not have forgotten that meal of whipped cream as something so utterly unimportant that it might never have existed? She began to think, more and more, to tell herself over and over again, to force herself to realise, that it was probably all finished, that Fabrice might never be anything for her now but a memory.

At the same time the few people she saw never failed when talking, as everybody talked then, about France, to emphasise that the French 'one knew', the families who were '*bien*', were all behaving very badly, convinced Pétainists. Fabrice was not one of them, she thought, she felt, but she wished she knew, she longed for evidence.

In fact, she alternated between hope and despair, but as the months went by without a word, a word that she was sure he could have sent if he had really wanted to, despair began to prevail.

Then, on a sunny Sunday morning in August, very early, her telephone bell rang. She woke up with a start, aware that it had been ringing already for several moments, and she knew with absolute certainty that this was Fabrice.

'Are you Flaxman 2815?'

'Yes.'

'I've got a call for you. You're through.'

'Allô – allô?'
'Fabrice?'
'Oui.'
'Oh! Fabrice – *on vous attend depuis si longtemps.*'
'*Comme c'est gentil. Alors, on peut venir tout de suite chez vous?*'
'Oh, wait – yes, you can come at once, but don't go for a minute, go on talking, I want to hear the sound of your voice.'
'No, no, I have a taxi outside, I shall be with you in five minutes. There's too much one can't do on the telephone, *ma chère, voyons –*'
Click.

She lay back, and all was light and warmth. Life, she thought, is sometimes sad and often dull, but there are currants in the cake and here is one of them. The early morning sun shone past her window on to the river, her ceiling danced with water-reflections. The Sunday silence was broken by two swans winging slowly upstream, and then by the chugging of a little barge, while she waited for that other sound, a sound more intimately connected with the urban love affair than any except the telephone bell, that of a stopping taxicab. Sun, silence, and happiness. Presently she heard it in the street, slowly, slower, it stopped, the flag went up with a ring, the door slammed, voices, clinking coins, footsteps. She rushed downstairs.

Hours later Linda made some coffee.

'So lucky,' she said, 'that it happens to be Sunday, and Mrs Hunt isn't here. What would she have thought?'

'Just about the same as the night porter at the Hotel Montalembert, I expect,' said Fabrice.

'Why did you come, Fabrice? To join General de Gaulle?'

'No, that was not necessary, because I have joined him already. I was with him in Bordeaux. My work has to be in France, but we have ways of communicating when we want to. I shall go and see him, of course, he expects me at midday, but actually I came on a private mission.'

He looked at her for a long time.

'I came to tell you that I love you,' he said, at last.

Linda felt giddy.

'You never said that to me in Paris.'

'No.'

'You always seemed so practical.'

'Yes, I suppose so. I had said it so often and often before in my life, I had been so romantic with so many women, that when I felt this to be different I really could not bring out all those stale old phrases again, I couldn't utter them. I never said I loved you, I never *tutoyé*'d you, on purpose. Because from the first moment I knew that this was as real as all the others were false, it was like recognising somebody – there, I can't explain.'

'But that is exactly how I felt too,' said Linda, 'don't try to explain, you needn't, I know.'

'Then, when you had gone, I felt I had to tell you, and it became an obsession with me to tell you. All those dreadful weeks were made more dreadful because I was being prevented from telling you.'

'How ever did you get here?'

'*On circule*,' said Fabrice, vaguely. 'I must leave again tomorrow morning, very early, and I shan't come back until the war is over, but you'll wait for me, Linda, and nothing matters so much now that you know. I was tormented, I couldn't concentrate on anything, I was becoming useless in my work. In future I may have much to bear, but I shan't have to bear you going away without knowing what a great great love I have for you.'

'Oh, Fabrice, I feel – well, I suppose religious people sometimes feel like this.'

She put her head on his shoulder, and they sat for a long time in silence.

Nancy Mitford: The Pursuit of Love

In the orchard

A splendid Midsummer shone over England: skies so pure, suns so radiant as were then seen in long succession, seldom favour, even singly, our wave-girt land. It was as if a band of Italian days had come from the South, like a flock of glorious passenger birds, and lighted to rest them on the cliffs of Albion. The hay was all got in; the fields round Thornfield were green and shorn; the roads white and baked; the trees were in their dark prime; hedge and wood, full-leaved and deeply tinted, contrasted well with the sunny hue of the clear meadows between.

On Midsummer-eve, Adèle, weary with gathering wild strawberries in Hay Lane half the day, had gone to bed with the sun. I watched her drop asleep, and when I left her I sought the garden.

It was now the sweetest hour of the twenty-four: – 'Day its fervid fires had wasted,' and dew fell cool on panting plain and scorched summit. Where the sun had gone down in simple state – pure of the pomp of clouds – spread a solemn purple, burning with the light of red jewel and furnace flame at one point, on one hill-peak, and extending high and wide, soft and still softer, over half heaven. The east had its own charm of fine, deep blue, and its own modest gem, a rising and solitary star: soon it would boast the moon; but she was yet beneath the horizon.

I walked a while on the pavement; but a subtle, well-known scent – that of cigar – stole from some window; I saw the library casement open a hand-breadth; I knew I might be watched thence; so I went apart into the orchard. No nook in the grounds more sheltered and more Eden-like; it was full of trees, it bloomed with flowers: a very high wall shut it out from the court, on one side; on the other, a beech avenue screened it from the lawn. At the bottom was a sunk fence; its sole separation from lonely fields: a winding walk, bordered with laurels and terminating in a giant horse-chesnut, circled at the base by a seat, led down to the fence. Here one could wander unseen. While such honey-dew fell, such silence reigned, such gloaming gathered, I felt as if I could haunt such shade for ever: but in threading the flower and fruit-parterres at the upper part of the inclosure, enticed there by the light the now-risen moon casts on this more open quarter, my step is stayed – not by sound, not by sight, but once more by a warning fragrance.

Sweet briar and southernwood, jasmine, pink, and rose, have long been yielding their evening sacrifice of incense: this new scent is neither of shrub nor flower; it is – I know it well – it is Mr Rochester's cigar. I look round and I listen. I see trees laden with ripening fruit. I hear a nightingale warbling in a wood half a mile off; no moving form is visible, no coming step audible; but that perfume increases: I must flee. I make for the wicket leading to the shrubbery, and I see Mr Rochester entering. I step aside into the ivy recess, he will not stay long: he will soon return whence he came, and if I sit still he will never see me.

But no – eventide is as pleasant to him as to me, and this antique garden as attractive; and he strolls on, now lifting the gooseberry-tree branches to look at the fruit, large as plums, with which they are laden; now taking a ripe cherry from the wall; now stooping towards a knot of flowers, either to inhale their fragrance or to admire the dew-beads on their petals. A great moth goes humming by me: it alights on a plant at Mr Rochester's foot: he sees it, and bends to examine it.

'Now, he has his back towards me,' thought I, 'and he is occupied too; perhaps, if I walk softly, I can slip away unnoticed.'

I trode on an edging of turf that the crackle of the pebbly gravel might not betray me: he was standing among the beds at a yard or two distant from where I had to pass; the moth apparently engaged him. 'I shall get by very well,' I meditated. As I crossed his shadow, thrown long over the garden by the moon, not yet risen high, he said quietly without turning:–

'Jane, come and look at this fellow.'

I had made no noise: he had not eyes behind – could his shadow feel? I started at first, and then I approached him.

'Look at his wings,' said he, 'he reminds me rather of a West Indian insect; one does not often see so large and gay a night-rover in England: there! he is flown.'

The moth roamed away. I was sheepishly retreating also; but Mr Rochester followed me, and when we reached the wicket, he said: –

'Turn back: on so lovely a night it is a shame to sit in the house; and surely no one can wish to go to bed while sunset is thus at meeting with moonrise.'

It is one of my faults, that though my tongue is sometimes prompt enough at an answer, there are times when it sadly fails me in framing an excuse; and always the lapse occurs at some crisis, when a facile word or plausible pretext is specially wanted to get me out of painful embarrassment. I did not like to walk at this hour alone with Mr Rochester in the shadowy orchard; but I could not find a reason to allege for leaving him. I followed with lagging step, and thoughts busily bent on discovering a means of extrication; but he himself looked so composed and so grave also, I became ashamed of feeling any confusion: the evil – if evil existent or prospective there was – seemed to lie with me only; his mind was unconscious and quiet.

'Jane,' he recommenced, as we entered the laurel walk, and slowly strayed down in the direction of the sunk fence and the horse-chesnut, 'Thornfield is a pleasant place in summer, is it not?'

'Yes, sir.'

'You must have become in some degree attached to the house, – you, who have an eye for natural beauties, and a good deal of the organ of Adhesiveness?'

'I am attached to it, indeed.'

'And though I don't comprehend how it is, I perceive you have acquired a degree of regard for that foolish little child Adèle, too; and even for simple dame Fairfax?'

'Yes, sir; in different ways, I have an affection for both.'

'And would be sorry to part with them?'

'Yes.'

'Pity!' he said, and sighed and paused. 'It is always the way of events in this life,' he continued presently: 'no sooner have you got settled in a pleasant resting-place, than a voice calls out to you to rise and move on, for the hour of repose is expired.'

'Must I move on, sir?' I asked. 'Must I leave Thornfield?'

'I believe you must, Jane. I am sorry, Janet, but I believe indeed you must.'

This was a blow: but I did not let it prostrate me.

'Well, sir, I shall be ready when the order to march comes.'

'It is come now – I must give it to-night.'

'Then you are going to be married, sir?'

'Ex-act-ly – pre-cise-ly: with your usual acuteness, you have hit the nail straight on the head.'

'Soon, sir?'

'Very soon, my – that is, Miss Eyre: and you'll remember, Jane, the first time I, or Rumour, plainly intimated to you that it was my intention to put my old bachelor's neck into the sacred noose, to enter into the holy estate of matrimony – to take Miss Ingram to my bosom, in short (she's an extensive armful: but that's not to the point – one can't have too much of such a very excellent thing as my beautiful Blanche): well, as I was saying – listen to me, Jane! You're not turning your head to look after more moths, are you? That was only a lady-clock, child, "flying away home." I wish to remind you that it was you who first said to me, with that discretion I respect in you – with that foresight, prudence and humility which befit your responsible and dependent position – that in case I married Miss Ingram – both you and little Adèle had better trot forthwith. I pass over the sort of slur conveyed in this suggestion on the character of my beloved; indeed, when you are far away, Janet, I'll try to forget it: I shall notice only its wisdom; which is such that I have made it my law of action. Adèle must go to school; and you, Miss Eyre, must get a new situation.'

'Yes, sir, I will advertise immediately: and meantime, I suppose' – I was going to say, 'I suppose I may stay here, till I find another shelter to betake myself to:' but I stopped, feeling it would not do to risk a long sentence, for my voice was not quite under command.

'In about a month I hope to be a bridegroom,' continued Mr Rochester; 'and in the interim I shall myself look out for employment and an asylum for you.'

'Thank you, sir; I am sorry to give' –

'Oh, no need to apologise! I consider that when a dependent does her duty as well as you have done yours, she has a sort of claim upon her employer for any little assistance he can conveniently render her; indeed I have already, through my future mother-in-law, heard of a place that I think will suit: it is to undertake the education of the five daughters of Mrs Dionysius O'Gall of Bitternutt Lodge, Connaught, Ireland. You'll like Ireland, I think: they're such warm-hearted people there, they say.'

'It is a long way off, sir.'

'No matter – a girl of your sense will not object to the voyage or the distance.'

'Not the voyage, but the distance: and then the sea is a barrier' –

'From what, Jane?'

'From England and from Thornfield: and' –

'Well?'

'From *you*, sir.'

I said this almost involuntarily; and, with as little sanction of free will, my tears gushed out. I did not cry so as to be heard, however; I avoided sobbing. The thought of Mrs O'Gall and Bitternutt Lodge struck cold to my heart; and colder the thought of all the brine and foam, destined, as it seemed, to rush between me and the master at whose side I now walked; and coldest the remembrance of the wider ocean – wealth, caste, custom intervened between me and what I naturally and inevitably loved.

'It is a long way,' I again said.

'It is, to be sure; and when you get to Bitternutt Lodge, Connaught, Ireland, I shall never see you again, Jane: that's morally certain. I never go over to Ireland, not having myself much of a fancy for the country. We have been good friends, Jane; have we not?'

'Yes, sir.'

'And when friends are on the eve of separation, they like to spend the little time that remains to them close to each other. Come – we'll talk over the voyage and the parting quietly, half an hour or so, while the stars enter into their shining life up in heaven yonder: here is the chesnut tree: here is the bench at its old roots. Come, we will sit there in peace to-night, though we should never more be destined to sit there together.' He seated me and himself.

'It is a long way to Ireland, Janet, and I am sorry to send my little friend on such weary travels: but if I can't do better, how is it to be helped? Are you anything akin to me, do you think, Jane?'

I could risk no sort of answer by this time: my heart was full.

'Because,' he said, 'I sometimes have a queer feeling with regard to you – especially when you are near me, as now: it is as if I had a string somewhere under my left ribs, tightly and inextricably knotted to a similar string situated in the corresponding quarter of your little frame. And if that boisterous channel, and two hundred miles or so of land come broad between us, I am afraid that cord of communion will be snapt; and then I've a nervous notion I should take to bleeding inwardly. As for you, – you'd forget me.'

'That I *never* should, sir: you know' – impossible to proceed.

'Jane, do you hear that nightingale singing in the wood? Listen!'

In listening, I sobbed convulsively; for I could repress what I endured no longer; I was obliged to yield, and I was shaken from head to foot with acute distress. When I did speak, it was only to express an impetuous wish that I had never been born, or never come to Thornfield.

'Because you are sorry to leave it?'

The vehemence of emotion, stirred by grief and love within me, was claiming mastery, and struggling for full sway; and asserting a right to predominate: to overcome, to live, rise, and reign at last; yes, – and to speak.

'I grieve to leave Thornfield: I love Thornfield: – I love it, because I have lived in it a full and delightful life, – momentarily at least. I have not been trampled on. I have not been petrified. I have not been buried with inferior minds, and excluded from every glimpse of communion with what is bright and energetic, and high. I have talked, face to face, with what I reverence; with what I delight in, – with an original, a vigorous, an expanded mind. I have known you, Mr Rochester; and it strikes me with terror and anguish to feel I absolutely must be torn from you for ever. I see the necessity of departure; and it is like looking on the necessity of death.'

'Where do you see the necessity?' he asked, suddenly.

'Where? You, sir, have placed it before me.'

'In what shape?'

'In the shape of Miss Ingram; a noble and beautiful woman, – your bride.'

'My bride! What bride? I have no bride!'

'But you will have.'

'Yes: – I will! – I will!' He set his teeth.

'Then I must go: – you have said it yourself.'

'No: you must stay! I swear it – and the oath shall be kept.'

'I tell you I must go!' I retorted, roused to something like passion. 'Do you think I can stay to become nothing to you? Do you think I am an automaton? – a machine without feelings? and can bear to have my morsel of bread snatched from my lips, and my drop of living water dashed from my cup? Do you think, because I am poor, obscure, plain, and little, I am soulless and heartless? You think wrong! – I have as much soul as you, – and full as much heart! And if God had gifted me with some beauty, and much wealth, I should have made it as hard for you to leave me, as it is now for me to leave you. I am not talking to you now through the medium of custom, conventionalities, or even of mortal flesh: – it is my spirit that addresses your spirit; just as if both had passed through the grave, and we stood at God's feet, equal, – as we are!'

'As we are!' repeated Mr Rochester – 'so,' he added, enclosing me in his arms, gathering me to his breast, pressing his lips on my lips: 'so, Jane!'

'Yes, so, sir,' I rejoined: 'and yet not so; for you are a married man – or as good as a married man, and wed to one inferior to you – to one with whom you have no sympathy – whom I do not believe you truly love; for I have seen and heard you sneer at her. I would scorn such a union: therefore I am better than you – let me go!'

'Where, Jane? To Ireland?'

'Yes – to Ireland. I have spoken my mind, and can go anywhere now.'

'Jane, be still; don't struggle so, like a wild, frantic bird that is rending its own plumage in its desperation.'

'I am no bird; and no net ensnares me; I am a free human being with an independent will; which I now exert to leave you.'

Another effort set me at liberty, and I stood erect before him.

'And your will shall decide your destiny,' he said: 'I offer you my hand, my heart, and a share of all my possessions.'

'You play a farce, which I merely laugh at.'

'I ask you to pass through life at my side – to be my second self and best earthly companion.'

'For that fate you have already made your choice, and must abide by it.'

'Jane, be still a few moments: you are over-excited: I will be still too.'

A waft of wind came sweeping down the laurel-walk, and trembled through the boughs of the chesnut: it wandered away – away – to an indefinite distance – it died. The nightingale's song was then the only voice of the hour: in listening to it, I again wept. Mr Rochester sat quiet, looking at me gently and seriously. Some time passed before he spoke: he at last said: –

'Come to my side, Jane, and let us explain and understand one another.'

'I will never again come to your side: I am torn away now, and cannot return.'

High Romance

'But, Jane, I summon you as my wife: it is you only I intend to marry.'

I was silent: I thought he mocked me.

'Come, Jane – come hither.'

'Your bride stands between us.'

He rose, and with a stride reached me.

'My bride is here,' he said, again drawing me to him, 'because my equal is here, and my likeness. Jane, will you marry me?'

Still I did not answer, and still I writhed myself from his grasp: for I was still incredulous.

'Do you doubt me, Jane?'

'Entirely.'

'You have no faith in me?'

'Not a whit.'

'Am I a liar in your eyes?' he asked passionately. "Little sceptic, you *shall* be convinced. What love have I for Miss Ingram? None: and that you know. What love has she for me? None: as I have taken pains to prove: I caused a rumour to reach her that my fortune was not a third of what was supposed, and after that I presented myself to see the result; it was coldness both from her and her mother. I would not – I could not – marry Miss Ingram. You – you strange – you almost unearthly thing! – I love as my own flesh. You – poor and obscure, and small and plain as you are – I entreat to accept me as a husband.'

'What me!' I ejaculated: beginning in his earnestness – and especially in his incivility – to credit his sincerity: 'me who have not a friend in the world but you – if you are my friend: not a shilling but what you have given me?'

'You, Jane. I must have you for my own – entirely my own. Will you be mine? Say yes, quickly.'

'Mr Rochester, let me look at your face: turn to the moonlight.'

'Why?'

'Because I want to read your countenance; turn!'

'There: you will find it scarcely more legible than a crumpled, scratched page. Read on: only make haste, for I suffer.'

His face was very much agitated and very much flushed, and there were strong workings in the features, and strange gleams in the eyes.

'Oh, Jane, you torture me!' he exclaimed. 'With that searching and yet faithful and generous look, you torture me!'

'How can I do that? If you are true and your offer real, my only feelings to you must be gratitude and devotion – they cannot torture.'

'Gratitude!' he ejaculated; and added wildly – 'Jane, accept me quickly. Say Edward – give me my name – Edward – I will marry you.'

'Are you in earnest? – Do you truly love me? – Do you sincerely wish me to be your wife?'

'I do; and if an oath is necessary to satisfy you, I swear it.'

'Then, sir, I will marry you.'

'Edward – my little wife!'

'Dear Edward!'

'Come to me – come to me entirely now,' said he: and added, in his deepest tone, speaking in my ear as his cheek was laid on mine, 'Make my happiness – I will make yours.'

'God pardon me!' he subjoined ere long, 'and man meddle not with me: I have her, and will hold her.'

'There is no one to meddle, sir. I have no kindred to interfere.'

'No – that is the best of it,' he said. And if I had loved him less I should have thought his accent and look of exultation savage: but sitting by him, roused from the nightmare of parting – called to the paradise of union – I thought only of the bliss given me to drink in so abundant a flow. Again and again he said, 'Are you happy, Jane?' and again and again I answered, 'Yes.' After which he murmured, 'It will atone – it will atone. Have I not found her friendless, and cold, and comfortless? Will I not guard, and cherish, and solace her? Is there not love in my heart, and constancy in my resolves? It will expiate at God's tribunal. I know my Maker sanctions what I do. For the world's judgment – I wash my hands thereof. For man's opinion – I defy it.'

But what had befallen the night? The moon was not yet set, and we were all in shadow: I could scarcely see my master's face, near as I was. And what ailed the chesnut tree? it writhed and groaned; while wind roared in the laurel walk, and came sweeping over us.

'We must go in,' said Mr Rochester: 'the weather changes. I could have sat with thee till morning, Jane.'

High Romance

'And so,' thought I, 'could I with you.' I should have said so, perhaps, but a livid, vivid spark leapt out of a cloud at which I was looking, and there was a crack, a crash, and a close rattling peal; and I thought only of hiding my dazzled eyes against Mr Rochester's shoulder.

The rain rushed down. He hurried me up the walk, through the grounds, and into the house; but we were quite wet before we could pass the threshold. He was taking off my shawl in the hall, and shaking the water out of my loosened hair, when Mrs Fairfax emerged from her room. I did not observe her at first, nor did Mr Rochester. The lamp was lit. The clock was on the stroke of twelve.

'Hasten to take off your wet things,' said he: 'and before you go, good-night – good-night, my darling!'

He kissed me repeatedly. When I looked up, on leaving his arms, there stood the widow, pale, grave, and amazed. I only smiled at her, and ran upstairs. 'Explanation will do for another time,' thought I. Still, when I reached my chamber, I felt a pang at the idea she should even temporarily misconstrue what she had seen. But joy soon effaced every other feeling; and loud as the wind blew, near and deep as the thunder crashed, fierce and frequent as the lightning gleamed, cataract-like as the rain fell during a storm of two hours' duration, I experienced no fear, and little awe. Mr Rochester came thrice to my door in the course of it, to ask if I was safe and tranquil: and that was comfort, that was strength for anything.

Before I left my bed in the morning, little Adèle came running in to tell me that the great horse-chestnut at the bottom of the orchard had been struck by lightning in the night, and half of it split away.

Charlotte Brontë: *Jane Eyre*

Balcony scene

JULIET. Three words, dear Romeo, and good night indeed.
   If that thy bent of love be honourable,
   Thy purpose marriage, send me word to-morrow,
   By one that I'll procure to come to thee,
   Where and what time thou wilt perform the rite;
   And all my fortunes at thy foot I'll lay,
   And follow thee my lord throughout the world.
NURSE [*within*]. Madam!
JULIET. I come, anon: – But if thou mean'st not well, I do beseech
   thee –
NURSE [*within*]. Madam!
JULIET. By and by, I come: –
   To cease thy suit, and leave me to my grief:
   To-morrow will I send.
ROMEO. So thrive my soul –
JULIET. A thousand times good night!

William Shakespeare: *Romeo and Juliet*

Hurt Feelings

Tom and Becky

When school broke up at noon, Tom flew to Becky Thatcher, and whispered in her ear:

'Put on your bonnet and let on you're going home; and when you get to the corner, give the rest of 'em the slip, and turn down through the lane and come back. I'll go the other way, and come it over 'em the same way.'

So the one went off with one group of scholars, and the other with another. In a little while the two met at the bottom of the lane, and when they reached the school they had it all to themselves. Then they sat together, with a slate before them, and Tom gave Becky the pencil and held her hand in his, guiding it, and so created another surprising house. When the interest in art began to wane, the two fell to talking. Tom was swimming in bliss. He said:

'Do you love rats?'

'No, I hate them!'

'Well, I do too – live ones. But I mean dead ones, to swing around your head with a string.'

'No, I don't care for rats much, anyway. What *I* like is chewing gum!'

'Oh, I should say so! I wish I had some now!'

'Do you? I've got some. I'll let you chew it awhile, but you must give it back to me.'

That was agreeable, so they chewed it turn about, and dangled their legs against the bench in excess of contentment.

'Was you ever at a circus?' said Tom.

'Yes, and my pa's going to take me again some time, if I'm good.'

'I been to the circus three or four times – lots of times. Church ain't shucks to a circus. There's things going on at a circus all the time. I'm going to be a clown in a circus when I grow up.'

Hurt Feelings

'Oh, are you! That will be nice. They're so lovely all spotted up.'

'Yes, that's so. And they get slathers of money – most a dollar a day, Ben Rogers says. Say, Becky, was you ever engaged?'

'What's that?'

'Why, engaged to be married.'

'No.'

'Would you like to?'

'I reckon so. I don't know. What is it like?'

'Like? Why, it ain't like anything. You only just tell a boy you won't ever have anybody but him, ever ever *ever*, and then you kiss, and that's all. Anybody can do it.'

'Kiss? What do you kiss for?'

'Why that, you know, is to – well, they always do that.'

'Everybody?'

'Why, yes, everybody that's in love with each other. Do you remember what I wrote on the slate?'

'Ye-yes.'

'What was it?'

'I shan't tell you.'

'Shall I tell *you*?'

'Ye-yes – but some other time.'

'No, now.'

'No, not now – tomorrow.'

'Oh, no, *now*, please, Becky. I'll whisper it, I'll whisper it ever so easy.'

Becky hesitating, Tom took silence for consent, and passed his arm about her waist and whispered the tale ever so softly, with his mouth close to her ear. And then he added:

'Now you whisper it to me – just the same.'

She resisted for a while, and then said:

'You turn your face away, so you can't see, and then I will. But you mustn't ever tell anybody – *will* you, Tom? Now you won't – *will* you?'

'No, indeed indeed I won't. Now Becky.'

He turned his face away. She bent timidly around till her breath stirred his curls, and whispered, 'I – love – you!'

Then she sprang away and ran around and around the desks and benches, with Tom after her, and took refuge in a corner at last,

Hurt Feelings

with her little white apron to her face. Tom clasped her about her neck and pleaded.

'Now Becky, it's all over – all over but the kiss. Don't you be afraid of that – it ain't anything at all. Please, Becky.'

And he tugged at the apron and the hands.

By and by she gave up and let her hands drop; her face, all glowing with the struggle, came up and submitted. Tom kissed the red lips and said:

'Now it's all done, Becky. And always after this, you know, you ain't ever to love anybody but me, and you ain't ever to marry anybody but me, never never and for ever. Will you?'

'No, I'll never love anybody but you, Tom and I'll never marry anybody but you, and you ain't to ever marry anybody but me, either.'

'Certainly. Of course. That's *part* of it. And always, coming to school, or when we're going home, you're to walk with me, when there ain't anybody looking – and you choose me and I choose you at parties, because that's the way you do when you're engaged.'

'It's so nice. I never heard of it before.'

'Oh it's ever so jolly! Why me and Amy Lawrence –'

The big eyes told Tom his blunder, and he stopped, confused.

'Oh, Tom! Then I ain't the first you've ever been engaged to!'

The child began to cry. Tom said:

'Oh, don't cry, Becky. I don't care for her any more.'

'Yes, you do, Tom – you know you do.'

Tom tried to put his arm about her neck, but she pushed him away and turned her face to the wall, and went on crying. Tom tried again, with soothing words in his mouth, and was repulsed again. Then his pride was up, and he strode away and went outside. He stood about, restless and uneasy, for a while, glancing at the door every now and then, hoping she would repent and come to find him. But she did not. Then he began to feel badly, and fear that he was in the wrong. It was a hard struggle with him to make new advances now, but he nerved himself to it and entered. She was still standing back there in the corner, sobbing with her face to the wall. Tom's heart smote him. He went to her and stood a moment, not knowing exactly how to proceed. Then he said, hesitatingly:

'Becky, I – I don't care for anybody but you.'

No reply – but sobs.
'Becky?' pleadingly.
'Becky, won't you say something?'
More sobs.

Tom got out his chiefest jewel, a brass knob from the top of an andiron, and passed it around her so that she could see it, and said:

'Please, Becky, won't you take it?'

She struck it to the floor. Then Tom marched out of the house and over the hills and far away, to return to school no more that day. Presently Becky began to suspect. She ran to the door; he was not in sight; she flew around to the play-yard; he was not there. Then she called:

'Tom! Come back, Tom!'

She listened intently, but there was no answer. She had no companions but silence and loneliness. So she sat down to cry again and upbraid herself, and by this time the scholars began to gather again, and she had to hide her grief and still her broken heart, and take up the cross of a long dreary aching afternoon, with none among the strangers about her to exchange sorrows with.

Mark Twain: *Tom Sawyer*

Disraeli's remonstrance

[Park Street. Thursday night, 7 February, 1839]
I wd have endeavoured to have spoken to you of that which it was necessary you shd know, & I wished to have spoken with the calmness which was natural to one humiliated & distressed. I succeeded so far as to be considered a 'selfish bully' & to be desired to quit your house for ever. I have recourse therefore to this miserable method of communicating with you; none can be more imperfect but I write as if it were the night before my execution . . .

I avow, when I first made my advances to you I was influenced by no romantic feelings. My father had long wished me to marry; my settling in life was the implied tho' not stipulated, condition of a disposition of his property, which wd have been convenient to me. I myself, about to commence a practical career, wished for the solace of a home, & shrunk from all the torturing passions of intrigue. I was not blind to worldly advantages in such an alliance, but I had already proved that my heart was not to be purchased. I found you in sorrow, & that heart was touched. I found you, as I thought, aimiable, tender, & yet acute & gifted with no ordinary mind – one whom I cd look upon with pride as the partner of my life, who cd sympathise with all my projects & feelings, console me in the moments of depression, share my hour of triumph, & work with me for our honor & happiness.

Now for your fortune: I write the sheer truth. That fortune proved to be much less than I, or the world, imagined. It was in fact, as far as I was concerned, a fortune which cd not benefit me in the slightest degree; it was merely a jointure not greater than your station required; enough to maintain your establishment & gratify your private tastes. To eat & to sleep in that house & nominally to call it mine – these cd be only objects for a penniless adventurer. Was this an inducement for me to sacrifice my sweet liberty, & that indefinite future wh: is one of the charms of existence? No, when months ago I told you there was only one link between us, I felt that my heart was inextricably engaged to you, & but for that I wd have terminated our acquaintance. From that moment I devoted to you all the passion of my being. Alas! It has been poured upon the sand . . .

By heavens as far as worldly interests are concerned, your aliance cd not benefit me. All that society can offer is at my command; it is not the apparent possession of a jointure that ever elevates position. I can live, as I live, without disgrace, until the inevitable progress of events gives me that independence which is all I require. I have entered into these ungracious details because you reproached me with my interested views. No; I wd not condescend to be the minion of a princess; and not all the gold of Ophir shd ever lead me to the altar. Far different are the qualities which I require in the sweet participator of my existence. My nature demands that my life shall be perpetual love.

Upon your general conduct to me I make no comment. It is now useless. I will not upbraid you. I will only blame myself . . . But you have struck deep. You have done that which my enemies have yet failed to do: you have broken my spirit. From the highest to the humblest scene of my life, from the brilliant world of fame to my own domestic hearth, you have poisoned all. I have no place of refuge: home is odious, the world oppressive.

Triumph – I seek not to conceal my state. It is not sorrow, it is not wretchedness; it is anguish, it is the *endurance* of that pang which is the passing characteristic of agony. All that can prostrate a man has fallen on my victim head. My heart outraged, my pride wounded, my honor nearly tainted. I know well that ere a few days can pass I shall be the scoff & jest of that world, to gain whose admiration has been the effort of my life. I have only one source of solace – the consciousness of self-respect. Will that uphold me? A terrible problem that must quickly be solved.

Farewell. I will not affect to wish you happiness for it is not in your nature to obtain it. For a few years you may flutter in some frivolous circle. But the time will come when you will sigh for any heart that could be fond and despair of one that can be faithful. Then will be the penal hour of retribution; then you will recall to your memory the passionate heart that you have forfeited, and the genius you have betrayed.

Benjamin Disraeli to Mary Anne Wyndham Lewis

Lord Reggie is offended

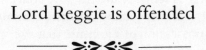

It was a romantic evening, and although Lord Reggie prided himself on being altogether impervious to the influences of Nature, he was not unaware that a warm and fantastic twilight may incline the average woman favourably to a suit that she might not be disposed to heed in the early morning, or during the garish sunshine of a summer afternoon. He presumed that Lady Locke was an average woman, simply because he considered all women exceedingly and distinctively average; and therefore, when he saw a soft expression steal into her dark face as she glanced at the faded turquoise of the sky, he decided to propose at once, and as prettily as possible. But Tommy was fussing about, wavy with childish excitement, and at first he could not speak.

'Tommy,' said Lady Locke at last, 'give me a kiss and run away to your supper. But, before you go, listen to me. Did you attend to Mr Amarinth's lecture?'

'Yes, yes, yes, mother! Of course, of course, of course,' cried Tommy, dancing violently on the lawn, and trying to excite Bung to a tempest.

'Well, remember that it was meant to be comic. It was only a nonsense lecture, like Edward Lear's nonsense books. Do you see? It was a turning of everything topsy-turvy. So what we have to do is just the opposite of everything Mr Amarinth advised. You understand, my boy?'

'All right, mumsy,' said Tommy. 'But I forget what he said.'

Lady Locke looked pleased, kissed his flushed little face, and packed him off.

'I hope the school children will do the same,' she said to Lord Reggie when he was gone. 'What a blessing a short memory can be!'

'Didn't you like the lecture, then?' Reggie asked. 'I thought it splendid, so full of imagination, so exquisitely choice in language and in feeling.'

'And so self-conscious.'

'Yes, as all art must be.'

'Art, art! You could make me hate that word!'

Reggie looked for once honestly shocked.

'You could hate art?' he said.

'Yes, if I could believe that it was the antagonist of Nature, instead of the faithful friend. No, I did not like the lecture, if one can like or dislike a mere absurdity. Tell me, Lord Reggie, are you self-consciously absurd?'

He drew his chair a little nearer to hers.

'I don't know,' he said; 'I hope I am beautiful. If I am beautiful, that is all I wish for. To be beautiful is to be complete. To be clever is easy enough. To be beautiful is so difficult, that even Byron had a club-foot with all his genius. Cleverness can be acquired. Hundreds of stupid people nowadays acquire the faculty of cleverness. That is why society is so boring. You find people practising mental scales and five-finger exercises at every party you go to. The true artist will never practise. How soft this twilight is, though not so delicate and subtle as that in Millet's *Angelus*. Lady Locke, I have something to tell you, and I will tell it to you now, while the stars come out, and the shadows steal from their homes in the trees. Esmé said today that marriage was a brilliant absurdity. Will you be brilliantly absurd? Will you marry me?'

He leaned forward, and took her hand rather negligently in his small and soft one. His face was calm, and he spoke in a clear and even voice. Lady Locke left her hand in his. She was quite calm too.

'I cannot marry you,' she said. 'Do you wish me to tell you why? Probably you do not; but I think I will tell you all the same. I am not brilliant, and therefore I have no wish to be absurd. If I married you I should be merely absurd without being brilliant at all. You do not love me. I think you love nothing. I like you; I am interested by you. Perhaps if you had a different nature I might even love you. But I can never love an echo, and you are an echo.'

'An echo is often more beautiful than the voice it repeats,' he said.

'But if the voice is quite ugly the echo cannot be beautiful,' she answered. 'I do not wish to be too frank, but as you have asked me to marry you I will say this. Your character seems to me to be an echo of Mr Amarinth's. I believe that he merely poses; but do those who imitate him merely pose? Do you merely pose? What Mr Amarinth really is it is quite impossible to tell. Perhaps there is nothing real about him at all. Perhaps, as he has said, his real man is only a Mrs Harris. He may be abnormal *au fond*; but you are not! What is your real self? Is it what I see, what I know?'

'Expression is my life,' Lord Reggie said in a rather offended voice, drawing away his hand. A red spot appeared in each of his cheeks. He began to realise that he was refused because he was not admired. It seemed almost incredible.

'Then the expression that I see is you?' she asked.

'I suppose so,' he replied, with a tinge of exceedingly boyish sulkiness.

'Then, till you have got rid of it never ask a woman to marry you. Men like you do not understand women. They do not try to;

Hurt Feelings

probably they could not if they did. Men like you are so twisted and distorted in mind that they cannot recognise their own distortion. It seems to me that Mr Amarinth has created a cult. Let me call it the cult of the green carnation. I suppose it may be called modern. To me it seems very silly and rather wicked. If you would take that hideous green flower out of your coat, not because I asked you to, but because you hated it honestly, I might answer your question differently. If you could forget what you call art, if you could see life at all with a straight, untrammelled vision, if you could be like a man, instead of like nothing at all in heaven or earth except that dyed flower, I might perhaps care for you in the right way. But your mind is artificially coloured: it comes from the dyer's. It is a green carnation; and I want a natural blossom to wear in my heart.'

She got up.

'You are not angry with me?' she asked.

Lord Reggie's face was scarlet.

'You talk very much like ordinary people,' he said, a little rude in his hurt self-love.

'I am ordinary,' she said. 'I am so glad of it . I think that after this week I shall try to be even more ordinary than I already am.'

Then she went slowly into the cottage.

Robert Hitchens: *The Green Carnation*

Fairy-Tale and Fantasy

Under the lee of the diamond mountain

July under the lee of the diamond mountain was a month of blanket nights and of warm, glowing days. John and Kismine were in love. He did not know that the little gold football (inscribed with the legend *Pro deo et patria et St Mida*) which he had given her rested on a platinum chain next to her bosom. But it did. And she for her part was not aware that a large sapphire which had dropped one day from her simple coiffure was stowed away tenderly in John's jewel box.

Late one afternoon when the ruby and ermine music room was quiet, they spent an hour there together. He held her hand and she gave him such a look that he whispered her name aloud. She bent towards him – then hesitated.

'Did you say "Kismine"?' she asked softly, 'or –'

She had wanted to be sure. She thought she might have misunderstood.

Neither of them had ever kissed before, but in the course of an hour it seemed to make little difference.

The afternoon drifted away. That night when a last breath of music drifted down from the highest tower, they each lay awake, happily dreaming over the separate minutes of the day. They had decided to be married as soon as possible.

                    F. Scott Fitzgerald: *The Diamond as big as the Ritz*

The fairy ring

Little Betsinda came in to put Gruffanuff's hair in papers; and the Countess was so pleased, that, for a wonder, she complimented Betsinda. 'Betsinda!' she said, 'you dressed my hair very nicely to-day; I promised you a little present. Here are five sh— no, here is a pretty little ring that I picked – that I have had some time.' And she gave Betsinda the ring she had picked up in the court. It fitted Betsinda exactly.

'It's like the ring the Princess used to wear,' says the maid.

'No such thing,' says Gruffanuff, 'I have had it this ever so long. There – tuck me up quite comfortable; and now, as it's a very cold night (the snow was beating in at the window) you may go and warm dear Prince Giglio's bed, like a good girl, and then you may unrip my green silk, and then you can just do me up a little cap for the morning, and then you can mend that hole in my silk stocking, and then you can go to bed, Betsinda. Mind, I shall want my cup of tea at five o'clock in the morning.'

'I suppose I had best warm both the young gentlemen's beds, ma'am,' says Betsinda.

Gruffanuff, for reply said, 'Hau-ah-ho! – Grau-haw-hoo! – Hong-hrho!' In fact, she was snoring sound asleep.

Her room, you know, is next to the King and Queen, and the Princess is next to them. So pretty Betsinda went away for the coals to the kitchen, and filled the Royal warming-pan.

Now, she was a very kind, merry, civil, pretty girl; but there must have been something very captivating about her this evening, for all the women in the servants' hall began to scold and abuse her. The housekeeper said she was a pert stuck-up thing: the upper-housemaid asked, how dare she wear such ringlets and ribbons, it was quite improper! The cook (for there was a woman-cook as well as a man-cook) said to the kitchen-maid that *she* never could see anything in that creetur: but as for the men, every one of them, Coachman, John, Buttons the page, and Monsieur, the Prince of Crim Tartary's valet, started up, and said –

'My eyes!
'O mussey!
'O jemmany!
'O ciel!
} What a pretty girl Betsinda is!'

'Hands off; none of your impertinence, you vulgar low people!' says Betsinda, walking off with her pan of coals. She heard the young gentlemen playing at billiards as she went upstairs: first to Prince Giglio's bed, which she warmed, and then to Prince Bulbo's room.

He came in just as she had done; and as soon as he saw her, 'O! O! O! O! O! O! what a beyou – oo – ootiful creature you are! You angel – you peri – you rosebud, let me be thy bulbul – thy Bulbo, too! Fly to the desert, fly with me! I never saw a young gazelle to glad me with its dark blue eye that had eyes like thine. Thou nymph of beauty, take, take this young heart. A truer never did itself sustain within a soldier's waistcoat. Be mine! Be mine! Be Princess of Crim Tartary! My Royal Father will approve our union; and, as for that little carroty-haired Angelica, I do not care a fig for her any more.'

'Go away, your Royal Highness, and go to bed, please,' said Betsinda, with the warming-pan.

But Bulbo said, 'No, never, till thou swearest to be mine, thou lovely, blushing chambermaid divine! Here, at they feet, the Royal Bulbo lies, the trembling captive of Betsinda's eyes.'

And he went on, making himself so *absurd and ridiculous*, that Betsinda, who was full of fun, gave him a touch with the warming-pan, which, I promise you, made him cry 'O-o-o-o!' in a very different manner.

Prince Bulbo made such a noise that Prince Giglio, who heard him from the next room, came in to see what was the matter. As soon as he saw what was taking place, Giglio, in a fury, rushed on Bulbo, kicked him in the rudest manner up to the ceiling, and went on kicking him till his hair was quite out of curl.

Poor Betsinda did not know whether to laugh or to cry; the kicking certainly must hurt the Prince, but then he looked so droll!

When Giglio had done knocking him up and down to the ground, and whilst he went into a corner rubbing himself, what do you think Giglio does? He goes down on his own knees to Betsinda, takes her hands, begs her to accept his heart, and offers to marry her that moment. Fancy Betsinda's condition, who had been in love with the Prince ever since she first saw him in the palace garden, when she was quite a little child.

'Oh, divine Betsinda!' says the Prince, 'how have I lived fifteen years in thy company without seeing thy perfections? What woman in all Europe, Asia, Africa, and America, nay, in Australia, only it is not yet discovered, can presume to be thy equal? Angelica? Pish! Gruffanuff? Phoo! The Queen? Ha, ha! Thou art my Queen. Thou art the real Angelica, because thou art really angelic.'

'Oh, Prince! I am but a poor chambermaid,' says Betsinda, looking, however, very much pleased.

'Didst thou not tend me in my sickness, when all forsook me?' continues Giglio. 'Did not thy gentle hand smooth my pillow, and bring me jelly and roast chicken?'

'Yes, dear Prince, I did,' says Betsinda, 'and I sewed your Royal Highness's shirt-buttons on too, if you please, your Royal Highness,' cries this artless maiden.

When poor Prince Bulbo, was was now madly in love with Betsinda, heard this declaration, when he saw the unmistakeable glances which she flung upon Giglio, Bulbo began to cry bitterly, and tore quantities of hair out of his head, till it all covered the room like so much tow.

Betsinda had left the warming-pan on the floor while the Princes were going on with their conversation, and as they began now to quarrel and be very fierce with one another, she thought proper to run away.

'You great big blubbering booby, tearing your hair in the corner there; of course you will give me satisfaction for insulting Betsinda. *You* dare to kneel down at Princess Giglio's knees and kiss her hand!'

'She's not Princess Giglio!' roars out Bulbo. 'She shall be Princess Bulbo; no other shall be Princess Bulbo.'

'You are engaged to my cousin!' bellows out Giglio.

'I hate your cousin,' says Bulbo.

'You shall give me satisfaction for insulting her!' cries Giglio in a fury.

'I'll have your life.'

'I'll run you through.'

'I'll cut your throat.'

'I'll blow your brains out.'

'I'll knock your head off.'

'I'll send a friend to you in the morning.'

'I'll send a bullet into you in the afternoon.'

'We'll meet again,' says Giglio, shaking his fist in Bulbo's face; and seizing up the warming-pan, he kissed it, because, forsooth, Betsinda had carried it, and rushed downstairs. What should he see on the landing but His Majesty talking to Betsinda, whom he called by all sorts of fond names. His Majesty had heard a row in the building, so he stated, and smelling something burning, had come out to see what the matter was.

'It's the young gentlemen smoking, perhaps, sir,' says Betsinda.

'Charming chambermaid,' says the King (like all the rest of them), 'never mind the young men! Turn thy eyes on a middle-aged autocrat, who has been considered not ill-looking in his time.'

'Oh, sir! what will Her Majesty say?' cries Betsinda.

'Her Majesty!' laughs the monarch. 'Her Majesty be hanged. Am I not Autocrat of Paflagonia? Have not I blocks, ropes, axes, hangmen – ha? Runs not a river by my palace wall? Have I not sacks to sew up wives withal? Say but the word, that thou wilt be mine own, – your mistress straightway in a sack is sewn, and thou the sharer of my heart and throne.'

When Giglio heard these atrocious sentiments, he forgot the respect usually paid to Royalty, lifted up the warming-pan, and knocked down the King as flat as a pancake; after which, Master Giglio took to his heels and ran away, and Betsinda went off screaming, and the Queen, Gruffanuff, and the Princess, all came out of their rooms. Fancy their feelings on beholding their husband, father, sovereign in this posture!

William Makepeace Thackeray: *The Rose and the Ring*

The courtship of the Yonghy-Bonghy-Bo

On the Coast of Coromandel
   Where the early pumpkins blow,
     In the middle of the woods
     Lived the Yonghy-Bonghy-Bo.
Two old chairs, and half a candle, –
One old jug without a handle, –
     These were all his worldly goods:
     In the middle of the woods,
     These were all the worldly goods
   Of the Yonghy-Bonghy-Bo,
   Of the Yonghy-Bonghy-Bo.

Once among the Bong-trees walking
   Where the early pumpkins blow,
     To a little heap of stones
     Came the Yonghy-Bonghy-Bo.
There he heard a Lady talking
To some milk-white hens of Dorking, –
     ' 'Tis the Lady Jingly Jones!
     On that little heap of stones
     Sits the Lady Jingly Jones!'
   Said the Yonghy-Bonghy-Bo.
   Said the Yonghy-Bonghy-Bo.

'Lady Jingly! Lady Jingly!
   Sitting where the pumpkins blow,
     Will you come and be my wife?'
   Said the Yonghy-Bonghy-Bo.
'I am tired of living singly, –

Fairy-tale and Fantasy

On this coast so wild and shingly, –
    I'm a-weary of my life;
  If you'll come and be my wife,
    Quite serene would be my life!' –
Said the Yonghy-Bonghy-Bo,
Said the Yonghy-Bonghy-Bo.

'On this Coast of Coromandel,
   Shrimps and watercresses grow,
    Prawns are plentiful and cheap,'
Said the Yonghy-Bonghy-Bo.
'You shall have my chairs and candle,
And my jug without a handle! –
    Gaze upon the Rolling deep
    (Fish is plentiful and cheap);
    As the sea, my love is deep!'
Said the Yonghy-Bonghy-Bo.
Said the Yonghy-Bonghy-Bo.

Lady Jingly answered sadly,
   And her tears began to flow, –
    'Your proposal comes too late,
  Mr Yonghy-Bonghy-Bo!
I would be your wife most gladly!'
(Here she twirled her fingers madly)
    'But in England I've a mate!
    Yes! you've asked me far too late,
    For in England I've a mate,
  Mr Yonghy-Bonghy-Bo!
  Mr Yonghy-Bonghy-Bo!

'Mr Jones – (his name is Handel, –
   Handel Jones, Esquire, & Co)
    Dorking fowls delights to send, –
  Mr Yonghy-Bonghy-Bo!
Keep, oh! keep your chairs and candle, –
And your jug without a handle, –
    I can merely be your friend!

Fairy-tale and Fantasy

    – Should my Jones more Dorkings send,
      I will give you three, my friend!
Mr Yonghy-Bonghy-Bo!
Mr Yonghy-Bonghy-Bo!

'Though you've such a tiny body,
    And your head so large doth grow, –
      Though your hat may blow away,
Mr Yonghy-Bonghy-Bo!
Though you're such a Hoddy Doddy –
Yet I wish that I could modi-
    fy the words I needs must say!
      Will you please to go away?
      That is all I have to say –
Mr Yonghy-Bonghy-Bo!
Mr Yonghy-Bonghy-Bo!'

Down the slippery slopes of Myrtle,
    Where the early pumpkins blow,
      To the calm and silent sea
    Fled the Yonghy-Bonghy-Bo.
There, beyond the Bay of Gurtle,
Lay a large and lively Turtle; –
    'You're the Cove', he said, 'for me;
      On your back beyond the sea,
      Turtle, you shall carry me!'
Said the Yonghy-Bonghy-Bo.
Said the Yonghy-Bonghy-Bo.

Through the silent-roaring ocean
    Did the Turtle swiftly go;
      Holding fast upon his shell
    Rode the Yonghy-Bonghy-Bo.
With a sad primeval motion
Towards the sunset isles of Boshen
    Still the Turtle bore him well.
      Holding fast upon his shell,
      'Lady Jingly Jones, farewell!'

Fairy-tale and Fantasy

Sang the Yonghy-Bonghy-Bo.
Sang the Yonghy-Bonghy-Bo.

From the Coast of Coromandel,
　　Did the Lady never go;
　　On the heap of stones she mourns
　　For the Yonghy-Bonghy-Bo.
On the Coast of Coromandel,
In his jug without a handle,
　　　Still she weeps, and daily moans;
　　　On that little heap of stones
　　　To her Dorking Hens she moans,
　　For the Yonghy-Bonghy-Bo.
　　For the Yonghy-Bonghy-Bo.

　　　　　　　　　　　　Edward Lear

The Top and the Ball

A Top and a Ball were lying close together in a drawer, among other playthings.

Thus said the Top to the Ball:

'Why should we not become bride and bridegroom, since we are thrown so much together?'

But the Ball, who was made of morocco leather, and fancied herself a very fashionable young lady, would not hear of such a proposal.

The next day, the little boy to whom the playthings belonged came to the drawer; he painted the Top red and yellow, and drove a brass nail through the middle of it; it was glorious after that to see the Top spin round.

'Look at me now!' said he to the Ball: 'what do you say to me now? Why should not we become man and wife? We suit each other so well – you can jump, and I can spin; it would be hard to find a couple happier than we should be.'

'Do you think so?' said the Ball; 'perhaps you do not know that my father and mother were morocco slippers, and that I have cork in my body.'

'Yes, but I am made of mahogany,' returned the Top; 'the Burgomaster manufactured me with his own hands; for he has a lathe of his own, and took great pleasure in turning me.'

'Can I trust you in this?' asked the Ball.

'May I never be whipped again if I lie,' said the Top.

'You don't talk amiss,' replied the Ball; 'but I am not at liberty, I am as good as betrothed to a young Swallow. Whenever I fly up in the air, he puts his head out of his nest and says, 'Will you marry me?' I have said 'Yes' to him in my heart, and that is almost the same as a betrothal. But one thing I promise you, I will never forget you!'

'That will be of great use!' quoth the Top, and no more was then said on the subject.

Next day the Ball was taken out. The Top saw it fly like a bird into the air – so high that it could be seen no longer; it came back again, but every time it touched the ground, it sprang higher than before. Either love, or the cork she had in her body, must have been the cause of this.

The ninth time she did not return; the boy sought and sought, but she was gone.

'I know well where she is,' sighed the Top; 'she is in the Swallow's nest, celebrating her wedding.' The more the Top thought of it, the more amiable did the Ball appear to him: that she could not be his only made his love the more vehement. Another had been preferred to him; he could not forget that! And the Top spinned and hummed, but was always thinking of the dear Ball who, in his imagination, grew more beautiful every moment. Thus passed several years – there was a constant love!

The Top was no longer young! however he was one day gilded all over; never before had he looked so handsome. He was now a gilt top, and spun most bravely, humming all the time yes, that was famous! But all at once he sprang too high and was gone! They sought and sought, even in the cellar; he was no where to be found.

Where was he?

Fairy-tale and Fantasy

He had jumped into a barrel full of all sorts of rubbish, cabbage-stalks sweepings, dust, etc, which had fallen in from the gutter.

'Alas! here I lie; my gay gilding will soon be spoiled; and what sort of trumpery can I have fallen in with?' And he peeped at a long cabbage-stalk which lay fearfully near him, and at a strange round thing somewhat like an apple; but it was not an apple, it was an old Ball, which had lain several years in the gutter, and was quite soaked through with water.

'Thank goodness! at last I see an equal, with whom I may speak,' said the Ball, looking fixedly at the gilt Top. 'I am made of real morocco, sewed together by a young lady's hands, and I have cork in my body; but I shall never again be noticed by anyone; I was on the point of marriage with the Swallow, when I fell into the gutter, and there I have lain five years, and am now wet through. Only think, what a wearisome time for a young lady to be in such a situation!'

But the Top answered not a word; he thought on his long-lamented companion, and the more he heard, the more certain he felt that it was she herself.

The servant-maid now came, and was going to turn the barrel over. 'Hurrah!' exclaimed she, 'there is the gilt Top.'

And the Top was brought back to the play-room; it was used and admired as before: but nothing more was heard of the Ball, nor did the Top ever again speak of his love for her; such a feeling must have passed away. How could it be otherwise, when he found that she had lain five years in the gutter, and that she was so much altered he scarcely knew her again when he met her in the barrel among rubbish?

Hans Andersen: *Danish Fairy-tales and Legends*

Royal Requests

Victoria and Albert

Tuesday, 15th October – Saw my dear Cousins come home quite safe from the Hunt, and charge up the hill at an immense pace. Saw Esterhazy. At about ½ p. 12 I sent for Albert; he came to the Closet where I was alone, and after a few minutes I said to him, that I thought he must be aware *why* I wished them to come here, – and that it would make me *too happy* if he would consent to what I wished (to marry me). We embraced each other, and he was *so* kind, *so* affectionate. I told him I was quite unworthy of him, – he said he would be very happy 'das Leben mit dir zu zubringen,' and was so kind, and seemed so happy, that I really felt it was the happiest brightest moment in my life. I told him it was a great sacrifice, – which he wouldn't allow; I then told him of the necessity of keeping it a secret, except to his father and Uncle Leopold and Stockmar, to whom he said he would send a Courier next day, – and also that it was to be as early as the beginning of February. I then told him to fetch Ernest, which he did and he congratulated us both and seemed very happy. I feel the happiest of human beings.

Queen Victoria's journal, 1839

Henry VIII and Mary of Guise

A royal marriage was not to be so speedily accomplished, though, and at this point events took an extraordinary turn. To the astonishment of French and English alike, Henry VIII announced that he, too, was a contender for the hand of Mary of Guise. The English

King had just lost his own third wife Jane Seymour, who had died not long after giving birth to a son, and his Council were urging him to marry again. The real reason for his unseemly haste was that he had just heard rumours of James V's plans.

James V [of Scotland] was Henry's nephew, but they were scarcely on the best of terms. Personal animosity apart, Henry had broken with Rome and had set himself up as head of the English Church. He was continually urging James to follow suit, but James remained obstinately faithful to the Pope. Worse still, James was an ardent supporter of Scotland's traditional alliance with France, an alliance which was a constant threat to England. Any further strengthening of the friendship between his northern and his southern neighbours was seen by Henry as a source of danger, and so he decided to stop the marriage at all costs. The simplest way to do so would be to marry James's bride himself.

When he heard that Mary would bring with her a dowry of 30,000 francs a year and was both 'lusty and fair', Henry wasted no more time. He told the French ambassador in London to let him know which French brides of suitable rank were available, and he made private investigations into Mary's wealth and lineage.

The ambassador duly conveyed the message to the French King, who was divided between amusement and indignation. The English must choose their wives as they did their horses, he observed: by lining them up and inspecting them. Although he was insulted by the implication that his own daughter should be included in this parade of prospective brides, he replied diplomatically enough. He would count it an honour if Henry chose a French wife, and he was welcome to select any lady in the kingdom – any lady, that is, except the Princess Margaret and except Mary of Guise, who was already promised elsewhere.

The negotiations between Henry and Francis now took on a distinctly farcical character. Catillon, the French ambassador, was summoned once more to Henry's presence. Knowing very well that monarch's unpredictable nature he was prepared for almost anything, but even he was shaken when Henry launched forth into impassioned declaration. So enamoured was he of Mary, Henry said, that he could consider no other bride, and he went on to elaborate this theme in considerable detail. When he eventually paused for breath, Castillon inquired tartly, 'Would you then marry another man's wife?'

Henry was not deterred. He had discovered, he said, that Mary had not yet given her personal consent to the match with James and was still available. Swallowing his exasperation, Castillon explained that Mary's father had full powers to act on her behalf. The marriage, could not have been contemplated had she been unwilling. Henry obstinately refused to believe this. Somewhat nonplussed, the ambassador ventured to inquire why Henry was so set on the Duke of Guise's daughter. With a knowing gleam in his eye, Henry retorted that Mary was big in person, and he had need of a big wife. 'I may be big in person,' observed Mary when they told her what he had said, 'but my neck is small!'

Rosalind K. Marshall: Mary of Guise

Henry V woos Katharine of France

KING HENRY. Fair Katharine, and most fair!
   Will you vouchsafe to teach a soldier terms
   Such as will enter at a lady's ear,
   And plead his love-suit to her gentle heart?
KATHARINE. Your majesty shall mock at me; I cannot speak your England.
KING HENRY. O fair Katharine, if you will love me soundly with your French heart, I will be glad to hear you confess it brokenly with your English tongue. Do you like me, Kate?
KATHARINE. *Pardonnez-moi*, I cannot tell vat is 'like me'.
KING HENRY. An angel is like you, Kate, and you are like an angel.
KATHARINE. *Que dit-il? que je suis semblable à les anges?*
ALICE. *Oui, vraiment, sauf votre grace, ainsi dit-il.*
KING HENRY. I said so, dear Katharine; and I must not blush to affirm it.

Royal Requests

KATHARINE. *O bon Dieu! les langues des hommes sont pleines de tromperies.*

KING HENRY. What says she, fair one? that the tongues of men are full of deceits?

ALICE. *Oui*, dat de tongues of de mans is be full of deceits – dat is de princess.

KING HENRY. The princess is the better Englishwoman. I'faith, Kate, my wooing is fit for thy understanding: I am glad thou canst speak no better English; for, if thou couldst, thou wouldst find me such a plain king, that thou wouldst think I had sold my farm to buy my crown. I know no ways to mince it in love, but directly to say, 'I love you': then, if you urge me further than to say, 'Do you in faith?' I wear out my suit. Give me your answer; i'faith, do; and so clap hands and a bargain: how say you, lady?

KATHARINE. *Sauf votre honneur*, me understand well.

KING HENRY. Marry, if you would put me to verses or to dance for your sake, Kate, why, you undid me; for the one I have neither words nor measure; and for the other, I have no strength in measure, yet a reasonable measure in strength. If I could win a lady at leap-frog, or by vaulting into my saddle with my armour on my back, under the correction of bragging be it spoken, I should quickly leap into a wife. Or if I might buffet for my love, or bound my horse for her favours, I could lay on like a butcher, and sit like a jack-an-apes, never off. But, before God, Kate, I cannot look greenly, nor gasp out my eloquence, nor I have no cunning in protestation; only downright oaths, which I never use till urged, nor never break for urging. If thou canst love a fellow of this temper, Kate, whose face is not worth sun-burning, that never looks in his glass for love of any thing he sees there, – let thine eye be thy cook. I speak to thee plain soldier: if thou canst love me for this, take me; if not, to say to thee that I shall die, is true, – but for thy love, by the Lord, no; yet I love thee too. And while thou livest, dear Kate, take a fellow of plain and uncoined constancy; for he perforce must do thee right, because he hath not the gift to woo in other places: for these fellows of infinite tongue, that can rime themselves into ladies' favours, they do always reason themselves out again. What! a speaker is but a prater; a rime is but a ballad. A good leg will fall; a straight back will stoop; a black beard will turn white; a curl'd pate will grow bald; a fair face will wither; a full eye will wax hollow; but a good heart, Kate, is the sun and the moon; or, rather, the sun, and not the moon, – for it shines bright, and never changes, but keeps his course truly. If thou would have such a one, take me: and take me, take a soldier; take a soldier, take a king: and what say'st thou, then, to my love? speak, my fair, and fairly, I pray thee.

KATHARINE. Is it possible dat I sould love de enemy of France?

KING HENRY. No; it is not possible you should love the enemy of France, Kate: but in loving me, you should love the friend of France; for I love France so well, that I will not part with a village of it; I will have it all mine: and, Kate, when France is mine and I am yours, then yours is France and you are mine.

KATHARINE. I cannot tell vat is dat.

KING HENRY. No, Kate? I will tell thee in French; which I am sure will hang upon my tongue like a new-married wife about her husband's neck, hardly to be shook off. *Je quand sur le possession de France, et quand vous avez le possession de moi,* – let me see, what then? Saint Denis be my speed! *donc votre est France et vous etes mienne.* It is as easy for me, Kate, to conquer the kingdom, as to speak so much more French: I shall never move thee in French, unless it be to laugh at me.

KATHARINE. *Sauf votre bonneur, le Francais que vous parlez, il est meilleur que l' Anglais lequel je parle.*

KING HENRY. No, faith, is't not, Kate: but thy speaking of my tongue, and I thine, most truly-false, must needs be granted to be much at one. But, Kate, dost thou understand thus much English, – Canst thou love me?

KATHARINE. I cannot tell.

KING HENRY. Can any of your neighbours tell, Kate? I'll ask them. Come, I know thou lovest me: and at night, when you come into your closet, you'll question this gentlewoman about me; and I know, Kate, you will to her dispraise those parts in me that you love with your heart: but, good Kate, mock me mercifully; the rather, gentle princess, because I love thee cruelly. If ever thou beest mine, Kate, – as I have a saving faith within me tells me thou shalt, – I get thee with scrambling, and thou must therefore needs prove a good soldier-breeder: shall not thou and I, between Saint Denis and Saint George, compound a boy, half French, half English, that shall go to Constantinople and take the Turk by the beard? shall we not? what say'st thou, my fair flower-de-luce?

KATHARINE. I do not know dat.

KING HENRY. No; 'tis hereafter to know, but now to promise: do but now promise, Kate, and you will endeavour for your French part of such a boy; and for my English moiety take the word of a king and a bachelor. How answer you, *la plus belle Katharine du monde, mon tres-chere et devin deesse?*

KATHARINE. Your majestee ave *fausse* French enough to deceive de most *sage demoiselle* dat is *en France.*

KING HENRY. Now, fie upon my false French! By mine honour, in true English, I love thee, Kate: by which honour I dare not swear thou lovest me; yet my blood begins to flatter me that thou dost, notwithstanding the poor and untempering effect of my visage. Now, beshrew my father's ambition! he was thinking of civil wars when he got me: therefore was I created with a stubborn outside, with an aspect of iron, that, when I come to woo ladies, I fright them. But, in faith, Kate, the elder I wax, the better I shall appear; my comfort is, that old age, that ill layer-up of beauty, can do no more spoil upon my face: thou hast me, if thou hast me, at the worst; and thou shalt wear me, if thou wear me, better and better: – and therefore tell me, most fair Katharine, will you have me? Put off your maiden blushes, avouch the thoughts of your heart with the looks of an empress; take me by the hand, and say, 'Harry of England, I am thine': which word thou shalt no sooner bless mine ear withal, but I will tell thee aloud, 'England is thine, Ireland is thine, France is thine, and Henry Plantagenet is thine'; who, though I speak it before his face, if he be not fellow with the best king, thou shalt find the best king of good fellows. Come, your answer in broken music, – for thy voice is music, and thy English broken; therefore, queen of all Katharines, break thy mind to me in broken English, – wilt thou have me?

KATHARINE. Dat is as it sall please de *roi mon père.*

KING HENRY. Nay, it will please him well, Kate, – it shall please him, Kate.

Royal Requests

KATHARINE. Den it sall also content me.
KING HENRY. Upon that I kiss your hand, and call you my queen.

William Shakespeare: *Henry V*

Advances to Attila

The sister of Valentinian was educated in the palace of Ravenna, and as her marriage might be productive of some danger to the state, she was raised, by the title of *Augusta*, above the hopes of the most presumptuous subject. But the fair Honoria had no sooner attained the sixteenth year of her age than she detested the importunate greatness which must for ever exclude her from the comforts of honourabe love; in the midst of vain and unsatisfactory pomp Honoria sighed, yielded to the impulse of nature, and threw herself into the arms of her chamberlain Eugenius. Her guilt and shame (such is the absurd language of imperious man) were soon betrayed by the appearances of pregnancy: but the disgrace of the royal family was published ·to the world by the imprudence of the Empress Placidia, who dismissed her daughter, after a strict and shameful confinement, to a remote exile at Constantinople. The unhappy princess passed twelve or fourteen years in the irksome society of the sisters of Theodosius and their chosen virgins, to whose *crown* Honoria could no longer aspire, and whose monastic assiduity of prayer, fasting and vigils she reluctantly imitated. Her impatience of long and hopeless celibacy urged her to embrace a strange and desperate resolution. The name of Attila was familiar and formidable at Constantinople, and his frequent embassies entertained a perpetual intercourse between his camp and the imperial palace. In the pursuit of love, or rather of revenge, the daughter of Placidia sacrificed every duty and every prejudice, and offered to deliver her person into the arms of a barbarian of whose language she was ignorant, whose figure was scarcely human, and whose religion and manners she abhorred. By the ministry of a

Royal Requests

faithful eunuch she transmitted to Attila a ring, the pledge of her affection, and earnestly conjured him to claim her as a lawful spouse to whom he had been secretly betrothed. These indecent advances were received, however, with coldness and disdain; and the king of the Huns continued to multiply the number of his wives till his love was awakened by the more forcible passions of ambition and avarice.

Edward Gibbon: *The Decline and Fall of the Roman Empire*

Proxy Proposals

Barkis is willin'

After we had jogged on for some little time, I asked the carrier if he was going all the way.

'All the way where?' inquired the carrier.

'There,' I said.

'Where's there?' inquired the carrier.

'Near London,' I said.

'Why that horse,' said the carrier, jerking the rein to point him out, 'would be deader than pork afore he got over half the ground.'

'Are you only going to Yarmouth then?' I asked.

'That's about it,' said the carrier. 'And there I shall take you to the stage-cutch, and the stage-cutch that'll take you to – wherever it is.'

As this was a great deal for the carrier (whose name was Mr Barkis) to say – he being, as I observed in a former chapter, of a phlegmatic temperament, and not at all conversational – I offered him a cake as a mark of attention, which he ate at one gulp, exactly like an elephant, and which made no more impression on his big face than it would have done on an elephant's.

'Did *she* make 'em, now?' said Mr Barkis, always leaning forward, in his slouching way, on the footboard of the cart with an arm on each knee.

'Peggotty, do you mean, sir?'

'Ah!' said Mr Barkis. 'Her.'

'Yes. She makes all our pastry and does all our cooking.'

'Do she though?' said Mr Barkis.

He made up his mouth as if to whistle, but he didn't whistle. He sat looking at the horse's ears, as if he saw something new there; and sat so, for a considerable time. By-and-by, he said:

'No sweethearts, I b'lieve?'

'Sweetmeats did you say, Mr Barkis?' For I thought he wanted something else to eat, and had pointedly alluded to that description of refreshment.

'Hearts,' said Mr Barkis. 'Sweethearts; no person walks with her!'

'With Peggotty?'

'Ah!' he said. 'Her.'

'Oh no. She never had a sweetheart.'

'Didn't she though?' said Mr Barkis.

Again he made up his mouth to whistle, and again he didn't whistle, but sat looking at the horse's ears.

'So she makes,' said Mr Barkis, after a long interval of reflection, 'all the apple parsties, and doos all the cooking, do she?'

I replied that such was the fact.

'Well. I'll tell you what,' said Mr Barkis. 'P'raps you might be writin' to her?'

'I shall certainly write to her,' I rejoined.

'Ah!' he said, slowly turning his eyes towards me. 'Well! If you was writin' to her, p'raps you'd recollect to say that Barkis was willin': would you?'

'That Barkis is willing,' I repeated, innocently. 'Is that all the message?'

'Yes–es,' he said, considering. 'Ye–es. Barkis is willin'.'

'But you will be at Blunderstone again tomorrow, Mr Barkis,' I said, faltering a little at the idea of my being far away from it then, 'and could give your own message so much better.'

As he repudiated this suggestion, however, with a jerk of his head, and once more confirmed his previous request by saying with profound gravity, 'Barkis is willin'. That's the message,' I readily undertook its transmission. While I was waiting for the coach in the hotel at Yarmouth that very afternoon, I procured a sheet of paper and an inkstand, and wrote a note to Peggotty which ran thus: 'My dear Peggotty. I have come here safe. Barkis is willing. My love to mamma. Yours affectionately. P.S. He says he particularly wants you to know – *Barkis is willing.*'

When I had taken this commission on myself prospectively, Mr Barkis relapsed into perfect silence; and I, feeling quite worn out by all that had happened lately, lay down on a sack in the cart and fell asleep.

Charles Dickens: *David Copperfield*

Bertie speaks for Gussie

How different it all would have been, I could not but reflect, if this girl had been the sort of girl one chirrups cheerily to over the telephone and takes for spins in the old two-seater. In that case, I would simply have said, 'Listen,' and she would have said, 'What?' and I would have said, 'You know Gussie Fink-Nottle,' and she would have said, 'Yes,' and I would have said, 'He loves you,' and she would have said either, 'What, that mutt? Well, thank heaven for one good laugh today!' or else, in more passionate vein, 'Hot dog! Tell me more.'

I mean to say, in either event the whole thing over and done with in under a minute.

But with the Bassett something less snappy and a good deal more glutinous was obviously indicated. What with all this daylight-saving stuff, we had hit the great open spaces at a moment when the twilight had not yet begun to cheese it in favour of the shades of night. There was a fag-end of sunset still functioning. Stars were beginning to peep out, bats were fooling round, the garden was full of the aroma of those niffy white flowers which only start to put in their heavy work at the end of the day – in short, the glimmering landscape was fading on the sight and all the air held a solemn stillness, and it was plain that this was having the worst effect on her. Her eyes were enlarged, and her whole map a good deal too suggestive of the soul's awakening for comfort.

Her aspect was that of a girl who was expecting something fairly fruity from Bertram.

In these circs., conversation inevitably flagged a bit. I am never at my best when the situation seems to call for a certain soupiness, and

I've heard other members of the Drones say the same thing about themselves. I remember Pongo Twistleton telling me that he was out in a gondola with a girl by moonlight once, and the only time he spoke was to tell her that old story about the chap who was so good at swimming that they made him a traffic cop in Venice.

Fell rather flat, he assured me, and it wasn't much later when the girl said she thought it was getting a little chilly and how about pushing back to the hotel.

So now, as I say, the talk rather hung fire. It had been all very well for me to promise Gussie that I would cut loose to this girl about aching hearts, but you want a cue for that sort of thing. And when, toddling along, we reached the edge of the lake and she finally spoke, conceive my chagrin when I discovered that what she was talking about was stars.

Not a bit of good to me.

'Oh, look,' she said. She was a confirmed Oh-looker. I had noticed this at Cannes, where she had drawn my attention in this manner on various occasions to such diverse objects as a French actress, a Provençal filling station, the sunset over the Estorels, Michael Arlen, a man selling coloured spectacles, the deep velvet blue of the Mediterranean, and the late Mayor of New York in a striped one-piece bathing suit. 'Oh, look at that sweet little star up there all by itself.'

I saw the one she meant, a little chap operating in a detached sort of way above a spinney.

'Yes,' I said.

'I wonder if it feels lonely.'

'Oh, I shouldn't think so.'

'A fairy must have been crying.'

'Eh?'

'Don't you remember? "Every time a fairy sheds a tear, a wee bit star is born in the Milky Way." Have you ever thought that, Mr Wooster?'

I never had. Most improbable, I considered, and it didn't seem to me to check up with her statement that the stars were God's daisy chain. I mean, you can't have it both ways.

However, I was in no mood to dissect and criticise. I saw that I had been wrong in supposing that the stars were not germane to the issue. Quite a decent cue they had provided, and I leaped on it promptly:

'Talking of shedding tears –'

But she was now on the subject of rabbits, several of which were messing about in the park to our right.

'Oh, look. The little bunnies!'

'Talking of shedding tears –'

'Don't you love this time of the evening, Mr Wooster, when the sun has gone to bed and all the bunnies come out to have their little suppers? When I was a child, I used to think that rabbits were gnomes, and that if I held my breath and stayed quite still, I should see the fairy queen.'

Indicating with a reserved gesture that this was just the sort of loony thing I should have expected her to think as a child, I returned to the point.

'Talking of shedding tears,' I said firmly, 'it may interest you to know that there is an aching heart in Brinkley Court.'

This held her. She cheesed the rabbit theme. Her face, which had been aglow with what I supposed was a pretty animation, clouded. She unshipped a sigh that sounded like the wind going out of a rubber duck.

'Ah, yes. Life is very sad, isn't it?'

'It is for some people. This aching heart, for instance.'

'Those wistful eyes of hers! Drenched irises. And they used to dance like elves of delight. And all through a foolish misunderstanding about a shark. What a tragedy misunderstandings are. That pretty romance broken and over just because Mr Glossop would insist that it was a flatfish.'

I saw that she had got the wires crossed.

'I'm not talking about Angela.'

'But her heart is aching.'

'I know it's aching. But so is somebody else's.'

She looked at me, perplexed.

'Somebody's else? Mr Glossop's, you mean?'

'No, I don't.'

'Mrs Travers's?'

The exquisite code of politeness of the Woosters prevented me clipping her one on the ear-hole, but I would have given a shilling to be able to do it. There seemed to me something deliberately fatheaded in the way she persisted in missing the gist.

'No, not Aunt Dahlia's, either.'

'I'm sure she is dreadfully upset.'

'Quite. But this heart I'm talking about isn't aching because of Tuppy's row with Angela. It's aching for a different reason altogether. I mean to say – dash it, you know why hearts ache!'

She seemed to shimmy a bit. Her voice, when she spoke, was whispery:

'You mean – for love?'

'Absolutely. Right on the bull's-eye. For love.'

'Oh, Mr Wooster!'

'I take it you believe in love at first sight?'

'I do, indeed.'

'Well, that's what happened to this aching heart. It fell in love at first sight, and ever since it's been eating itself out, as I believe the expression is.'

There was a silence. She had turned away and was watching a duck out on the lake. It was tucking into weeds, a thing I've never been able to understand anyone wanting to do. Though I suppose, if you face it squarely, they're no worse than spinach. She stood drinking it in for a bit, and then it suddenly stood on its head and disappeared, and this seemed to break the spell.

'Oh, Mr Wooster!' she said again, and from the tone of her voice, I could see that I had got her going.

'For you, I mean to say,' I proceeded, starting to put in the fancy touches. I dare say you have noticed on these occasions that the difficulty is to plant the main idea, to get the general outline of the thing well fixed. The rest is mere detail work. I don't say I became glib at this juncture, but I certainly became a dashed sight glibber than I had been.

'It's having the dickens of a time. Can't eat, can't sleep – all for love of you. And what makes it all so particularly rotten is that it – this aching heart – can't bring itself up to the scratch and tell you the position of affairs, because your profile has gone and given it cold feet. Just as it is about to speak, it catches sight of you sideways, and words fail it. Silly, of course, but there it is.'

Proxy Proposals

I heard her give a gulp, and I saw that her eyes had become moistish. Drenched irises, if you care to put it that way.

'Lend you a handkerchief?'

'No, thank you. I'm quite all right.'

It was more than I could say for myself. My efforts had left me weak. I don't know if you suffer in the same way, but with me the act of talking anything in the nature of real mashed potatoes always induces a sort of prickly sensation and a hideous feeling of shame, together with a marked starting of the pores.

I remember at my Aunt Agatha's place in Hertfordshire once being put on the spot and forced to enact the role of King Edward III saying good-bye to that girl of his, Fair Rosamund, at some sort of pageant in aid of the Distressed Daughters of the Clergy. It involved some rather warmish medieval dialogue, I recall, racy of the days when they called a spade a spade, and by the time the whistle blew, I'll bet no Daughter of the Clergy was half as distressed as I was. Not a dry stitch.

My reaction now was very similar. It was a highly liquid Bertram who, hearing his *vis-à-vis* give a couple of hiccups and start to speak, bent an attentive ear.

'Please don't say any more, Mr Wooster.'

Well, I wasn't going to, of course.

'I understand.'

I was glad to hear this.

'Yes, I understand. I won't be so silly as to pretend not to know what you mean. I suspected this at Cannes, when you used to stand and stare at me without speaking a word, but with whole volumes in your eyes.'

If Angela's shark had bitten me in the leg, I couldn't have leaped more convulsively. So tensely had I been concentrating on Gussie's interests that it hadn't so much as crossed my mind that another and an unfortunate construction could be placed on those words of mine. The persp., already bedewing my brow, became a regular Niagara.

My whole fate hung upon a woman's word. I mean to say, I couldn't back out. If a girl thinks a man is proposing to her, and on that understanding books him up, he can't explain to her that she has got hold of entirely the wrong end of the stick and that he hadn't the smallest intention of suggesting anything of the kind. He must simply let it ride. And the thought of being engaged to a girl who talked openly about fairies being born because stars blew their noses, or whatever it was, frankly appalled me.

She was carrying on with her remarks, and as I listened I clenched my fists till I shouldn't wonder if the knuckles didn't stand out white under the strain. It seemed as if she would never get to the nub.

'Yes, all through those days at Cannes I could see what you were trying to say. A girl always knows. And then you followed me down here, and there was that same dumb, yearning look in your eyes when we met this evening. And then you were so insistent that I should come out and walk with you in the twilight. And now you stammer out those halting words. No, this does not come as a surprise. But I am sorry –'

The word was like one of Jeeves's pick-me-ups. Just as if a glassful of meat sauce, red pepper, and the yolk of an egg – though, as I say, I am convinced that these are not the sole ingredients – had been shot into me, I expanded like some lovely flower blossoming in the sunshine. It was all right, after all. My guardian angel had not been asleep at the switch.

'– but I am afraid it is impossible.'

She paused.

'Impossible,' she repeated.

I had been so busy feeling saved from the scaffold that I didn't get on to it for a moment that an early reply was desired.

'Oh, right ho,' I said hastily.

'I'm sorry.'

'Quite all right.'

'Sorrier than I can say.'

'Don't give it another thought.'

'We can still be friends.'

'Oh, rather.'

'Then shall we just say no more about it; keep what has happened as a tender little secret between ourselves?'

'Absolutely.'

'We will. Like something lovely and fragrant laid away in lavender.'

'In lavender – right.'

There was a longish pause. She was gazing at me in a divinely pitying sort of way, much as if I had been a snail she had happened accidentally to bring her short French vamp down on, and I longed to tell her that it was all right, and that Bertram, so far from being the victim of despair, had never felt fizzier in his life. But, of course, one can't do that sort of thing. I simply said nothing, and stood there looking brave.

'I wish I could,' she murmured.

'Could?' I said, for my attensh had been wandering.

'Feel towards you as you would like me to feel.'

'Oh, ah.'

'But I can't. I'm sorry.'

'Absolutely O.K. Faults on both sides, no doubt.'

'Because I am fond of you, Mr – no, I think I must call you Bertie. May I?'

'Oh, rather.'

'Because we are real friends.'

'Quite.'

'I do like you, Bertie. And if things were different – I wonder –'

'Eh?'

'After all, we are real friends . . . We have this common memory . . . You have a right to know . . . I don't want you to think – Life is such a muddle, isn't it?'

To many men, no doubt, these broken utterances would have appeared mere drooling and would have been dismissed as such. But the Woosters are quicker-witted than the ordinary and can read between the lines. I suddenly divined what it was that she was trying to get off the chest.

'You mean there's someone else?'

She nodded.

'You're in love wth some other bloke?'

She nodded.

'Engaged, what?'

This time she shook the pumpkin.

'No, not engaged.'

Well, that was something, of course. Nevertheless, from the way she spoke, it certainly looked as if poor old Gussie might as well scratch his name off the entry list, and I didn't at all like the prospect of having to break the bad news to him. I had studied the man closely, and it was my conviction that this would about be his finish.

Gussie, you see, wasn't like some of my pals – the name of Bingo Little is one that springs to the lips – who, if turned down by a girl, would simply say, 'Well, bung-ho!' and toddle off quite happily to find another. He was so manifestly a bird who, having failed to score in the first chukker, would turn the thing up and spend the rest of his life brooding over his newts and growing long grey whiskers, like one of those chaps you read about in novels, who live in the great white house you can just see over there through the trees and shut themselves off from the world and have pained faces.

'I'm afraid he doesn't care for me in that way. At least, he has said nothing. You understand that I am only telling you this because –'

'Oh, rather.'

'It's odd that you should have asked me if I believed in love at first sight.' She half-closed her eyes. '"Who ever loved that loved not at first sight?"' she said in a rummy voice that brought back to me – I don't know why – the picture of my Aunt Agatha, as Boadicea, reciting at that pageant I was speaking of. 'It's a silly little story. I was staying with some friends in the country, and I had gone for a walk with my dog, and the poor wee mite got a nasty thorn in his little foot and I didn't know what to do. And then suddenly this man came along –'

Harking back once again to that pageant, in sketching out for you my emotions on that occasion, I showed you only the darker side of the picture. There was, I should now mention, a splendid aftermath when, having climbed out of my suit of chain mail and sneaked off to the local pub, I entered the saloon bar and requested mine host to start pouring. A moment later, a tankard of their special home-brewed was in my hand, and the ecstasy of that first gollup is still green in my memory. The recollection of the agony through which I had passed was just what was needed to make it perfect.

It was the same now. When I realised, listening to her words, that she must be referring to Gussie – I mean to say, there couldn't have been a whole platoon of men taking thorns out of her dog that day; the animal wasn't a pin-cushion – and became aware that Gussie,

Proxy Proposals

who an instant before had, to all appearances, gone so far back in the betting as not to be worth a quotation, was the big winner after all, a positive thrill permeated the frame and there escaped my lips a 'Wow!' so crisp and hearty that the Bassett leaped a liberal inch and a half from terra firma.

'I beg your pardon?' she said.

I waved a jaunty hand.

'Nothing,' I said. 'Nothing. Just remembered there's a letter I have to write tonight without fail. If you don't mind, I think I'll be going in. Here,' I said, 'comes Gussie Fink-Nottle. He will look after you.'

And, as I spoke, Gussie came sidling out from behind a tree.

I passed away and left them to it. As regards these two, everything was beyond a question absolutely in order. All Gussie had to do was keep his head down and not press. Already, I felt, as I legged it back to the house, the happy ending must have begun to function. I mean to say, when you leave a girl and a man, each of whom has admitted in set terms that she and he loves him and her, in close juxtaposition in the twilight, there doesn't seem much more to do but start pricing fish slices.

Something attempted, something done, seemed to me to have earned two-penn'orth of wassail in the smoking-room.

I proceeded thither.

P. G. Wodehouse: *Right ho, Jeeves*

Reconciliations and Reunions

Gabriel and Bathsheba

Bathsheba went home, her mind occupied with a new trouble, which being rather harassing than deadly was calculated to do good by diverting her from the chronic gloom of her life. She was set thinking a great deal about Oak and of his wish to shun her; and there occurred to Bathsheba several incidents of her latter intercourse with him, which, trivial when singly viewed, amounted together to a perceptible disinclination for her society. It broke upon her at length as a great pain that her last old disciple was about to forsake her and flee. He who had believed in her and argued on her side when all the rest of the world was against her, had at last like the others become weary and neglectful of the old cause, and was leaving her to fight her battles alone.

Three weeks went on, and more evidence of his want of interest in her was forthcoming. She noticed that instead of entering the small parlour or office where the farm accounts were kept, and waiting, or leaving a memorandum as he had hitherto done during her seclusion, Oak never came at all when she was likely to be there, only entering at unseasonable hours when her presence in that part of the house was least to be expected. Whenever he wanted direction he sent a message, or note with neither heading nor signature, to which she was obliged to reply in the same off-hand style. Poor Bathsheba began to suffer now from the most torturing sting of all – a sensation that she was despised.

The autumn wore away gloomily enough amid these melancholy conjectures, and Christmas-day came, completing a year of her legal widowhood, and two years and a quarter of her life alone. On examining her heart it appeared beyond measure strange that the subject of which the season might have been supposed suggestive – the event in the hall at Boldwood's – was not agitating her at all; but instead, an agonising conviction that everybody abjured her – for what she could not tell – and that Oak was the ringleader of the recusants. Coming out of church that day she looked round in hope that Oak, whose bass voice she had heard rolling out from the gallery overhead in a most unconcerned manner, might chance to linger in her path in the old way. There he was as usual, coming down the path behind her. But on seeing Bathsheba turn, he looked aside, and as soon as he got beyond the gate, and there was the barest excuse for a divergence, he made one, and vanished.

The next morning brought the culminating stroke; she had been expecting it long. It was a formal notice by letter from him that he should not renew his engagement with her for the following Lady-day.

Bathsheba actually sat and cried over this letter most bitterly. She was aggrieved and wounded that the possession of hopeless love from Gabriel, which she had grown to regard as her inalienable right for life, should have been withdrawn just at his own pleasure in this way. She was bewildered too by the prospect of having to rely on her own resources again: it seemed to herself that she never could again acquire energy sufficient to go to market, barter, and sell. Since Troy's death Oak had attended all sales and fairs for her, transacting her business at the same time with his own. What should she do now? Her life was becoming a desolation.

So desolate was Bathsheba this evening, that in an absolute hunger for pity and sympathy, and miserable in that she appeared to have outlived the only true friendship she had ever owned, she put on her bonnet and cloak and went down to Oak's house just after sunset, guided on her way by the pale primrose rays of a crescent moon a few days old.

A lively firelight shone from the window, but nobody was visible in the room. She tapped nervously, and then thought it doutbful if it were right for a single woman to call upon a bachelor who lived alone, although he was her manager, and she might be supposed to call on business without any real impropriety. Gabriel opened the door, and the moon shone upon his forehead.

'Mr Oak,' said Bathsheba faintly.

'Yes; I am Mr Oak,' said Gabriel. 'Who have I the honour – O how stupid of me, not to know you, mistress!'

'I shall not be your mistress much longer, shall I, Gabriel?' she said in pathetic tones.

'Well, no. I suppose – But come in, ma'am. Oh – and I'll get a light,' Oak replied, with some awkwardness.

'No; not on my account.'

'It is so seldom that I get a lady visitor that I'm afraid I haven't proper accommodation. Will you sit down, please? Here's a chair, and there's one, too. I am sorry that my chairs all have wood seats, and are rather hard, but I – was thinking of getting some new ones.' Oak placed two or three for her.

'They are quite easy enough for me.'

So down she sat, and down he sat, the fire dancing in their faces, and upon the old furniture,

> all a-sheenen
> Wi' long years o' handlen,

that formed Oak's array of household possessions, which sent back a dancing reflection in reply. It was very odd to these two persons, who knew each other passing well, that the mere circumstance of their meeting in a new place and in a new way should make them so awkward and constrained. In the fields, or at her house, there had never been any embarrassment; but now that Oak had become the entertainer their lives seemed to be moved back again to the days when they were strangers.

'You'll think it strange that I have come, but –'

'O no; not at all.'

'But I thought – Gabriel, I have been uneasy in the belief that I have offended you, and that you are going away on that account. It grieved me very much, and I couldn't help coming.'

'Offended me! As if you could do that, Bathsheba!'

'Haven't I?' she asked, gladly. 'But, what are you going away for else?'

'I am not going to emigrate, you know; I wasn't aware that you would wish me not to when I told 'ee, or I shouldn't have thought of doing it,' he said, simply. 'I have arranged for Little Weatherbury Farm, and shall have it in my own hands at Lady-day. You know I've had a share in it for some time. Still, that wouldn't prevent my attending to your business as before, hadn't it been that things have been said about us.'

'What?' said Bathsheba in surprise. 'Things said about you and me. What are they?'

'I cannot tell you.'

'It would be wiser if you were to, I think. You have played the part of mentor to me many times, and I don't see why you should fear to do it now.'

'It is nothing that you have done, this time. The top and tail o't is this – that I'm sniffing about here, and waiting for poor Boldwood's farm, with a thought of getting you some day.'

'Getting me! What does that mean?'

'Marrying of 'ee, in plain British. You asked me to tell, so you mustn't blame me.'

Bathsheba did not look quite so alarmed as if a cannon had been discharged by her ear, which was what Oak had expected. 'Marrying me! I didn't know it was that you meant,' she said, quietly. 'Such a thing as that is too absurd – too soon – to think of, by far!'

'Yes; of course, it is too absurd. I don't desire any such thing; I should think that was plain enough by this time. Surely, surely you be the last person in the world I think of marrying. It is too absurd, as you say.'

'"Too – s-s-soon" were the words I used.'

'I must beg your pardon for correcting you, but you said, "too absurd", and so do I.'

'I beg your pardon too!' she returned, with tears in her eyes. '"Too soon" was what I said. But it doesn't matter a bit – not at all – but I only meant, "too soon". Indeed, I didn't, Mr Oak, and you must believe me!'

Gabriel looked her long in the face, but the firelight being faint there was not much to be seen. 'Bathsheba,' he said, tenderly and in surprise, and coming closer: 'If I only knew one thing – whether you would allow me to love you and win you, and marry you after all – if I only knew that!'

'But you never will know,' she murmured.

'Why?'

'Because you never ask.'

Reconciliations and Reunions

'Oh – Oh!' said Gabriel, with a low laugh of joyousness. 'My own dear –'

'You ought not to have sent me that harsh letter this morning,' she interrupted. 'It shows you didn't care a bit about me, and were ready to desert me like all the rest of them! It was very cruel of you, considering I was the first sweetheart that you ever had, and you were the first I ever had; and I shall not forget it!'

'Now, Bathsheba, was ever anybody so provoking?' he said, laughing. 'You know it was purely that I, as an unmarried man, carrying on a business for you as a very taking young woman, had a proper hard part to play – more particular that people knew I had a sort of feeling for 'ee; and I fancied, from the way we were mentioned together, that it might injure your good name. Nobody knows the heat and fret I have been caused by it.'

'And was that all?'

'All.'

'O, how glad I am I came!' she exclaimed, thankfully, as she rose from her seat. 'I have thought so much more of you since I fancied you did not want even to see me again. But I must be going now, or I shall be missed. Why, Gabriel,' she said, with a slight laugh, as they went to the door, 'it seems exactly as if I had come courting you – how dreadful!'

'And quite right, too,' said Oak. 'I've danced at your skittish heels, my beautiful Bathsheba, for many a long mile, and many a long day; and it is hard to begrudge me this one visit . . .'

Thomas Hardy: *Far from the Madding Crowd*

Below stairs

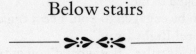

The basement door opened, and Kipps came into the kitchen. He was flushed and panting.

He struggled for speech.

''Ere,' he said, and held out two half-sixpences.

Reconciliations and Reunions

Ann stood behind the kitchen table – face pale and eyes round, and now – and it simplified Kipps very much – he could see she had indeed been crying.

'Well?' she said.

'Don't you see?'

Ann moved her head slightly.

'I kep' it all these years.'

'You kep' it too long.'

His mouth closed and his flush died away. He looked at her. The amulet, it seemed, had failed to work.

'Ann!' he said.

'Well?'

'Ann.'

The conversation still hung fire.

'Ann,' he said; made a movement with his hands that suggested appeal and advanced a step.

Ann shook her head more definitely, and became defensive.

'Look here, Ann,' said Kipps. 'I been a fool.'

They stared into each other's miserable eyes.

'Ann,' he said. 'I want to marry you.'

Ann clutched the table edge. 'You can't,' she said faintly.

He made as if to approach her round the table, and she took a step that restored their distance.

'I must,' he said.

'You can't.'

'I must. You *got* to marry me, Ann.'

'You can't go marrying everybody. You got to marry '*er*.'

'I shan't.'

Ann shook her head. 'You're engaged to that girl. Lady, rather. You can't be engaged to me.'

'I don't want to be engaged to you. I *been* engaged. I want to be married to you. See? Right away.'

Ann turned a shade paler. 'But what d'you mean?' she asked.

'Come right off to London and marry me. Now.'

'What d'you mean?'

Kipps became extremely lucid and earnest.

'I mean, come right off and marry me now before any one else can. See?'

'In London?'

'In London.'

They stared at one another again. They took things for granted in the most amazing way.

'I couldn't,' said Ann. 'For one thing, my month's not up for mor'n free weeks yet.'

They hung before that for a moment as though it was insurmountable.

'Look 'ere, Ann! Arst to go. Arst to go!'

'*She* wouldn't,' said Ann.

'Then come without arsting,' said Kipps.

'She'd keep my box –'

'She won't.'

'She will.'

'She won't.'

'You don't know 'er.'

'Well, desh 'er – let 'er! LET 'ER! Who cares? I'll buy you a 'undred boxes if you'll come.'

'It wouldn't be right towards Her.'

'It isn't Her you got to think about, Ann. It's me.'

'And you 'aven't treated me properly,' she said. 'You 'aven't treated me properly, Artie. You didn't ought to 'ave –'

'I didn't say I 'ad,' he interrupted, 'did I? Ann,' he appealed, 'I didn't come to arguefy. I'm all wrong. I never said I wasn't. It's yes or no. Me or not . . . I been a fool. There! See? I been a fool. Ain't that enough? I got myself all tied up with everyone and made a fool of myself all round . . .'

He pleaded, 'It isn't as if we didn't care for one another, Ann.'

She seemed impassive, and he resumed his discourse.

'I thought I wasn't likely ever to see you again, Ann. I reely did. It isn't as though I was seein' you all the time. I didn't know what I wanted, and I went and be'aved like a fool – jest as any one might. I know what I want, and I know what I don't want now.

'Ann!'

'Well?'

'Will you come? . . . Will you come? . . .'

Silence.

'If you don't answer me, Ann – I'm desprit – if you don't

Reconciliations and Reunions

answer me now, if you don't say you'll come, I'll go right out now – '

He turned doorward passionately as he spoke, with his threat incomplete.

'I'll go,' he said. 'I 'aven't a friend in the world! I been and throwed everything away. I don't know why I done things and why I 'aven't. All I know is I can't stand nothing in the world any more.' He choked. 'The pier,' he said.

He fumbled with the door-latch, grumbling some inarticulate self-pity, as if he sought a handle, and then he had it open.

Clearly he was going.

'Artie!' said Ann sharply.

He turned about, and the two hung white and tense.

'I'll do it,' said Ann.

His face began to work, he shut the door and came a step back to her, staring; his face became pitiful, and then suddenly they moved together. 'Artie!' she cried, 'don't go!' and held out her arms, weeping.

They clung close to one another . . .

'Oh, I *been* so mis'bel!' cried Kipps, clinging to this lifebuoy; and suddenly his emotion, having no further serious work in hand, burst its way to a loud *boohoo!* His fashionable and expensive gibus flopped off, and fell and rolled and lay neglected on the floor.

'I been so mis'bel,' said Kipps, giving himself vent. 'Oh, I *been* so mis'bel, Ann!'

'Be quiet,' said Ann, holding his poor blubbering head tightly to her heaving shoulder, herself all a-quiver; 'be quiet. She's there! Listenin'. She'll 'ear you, Artie on the stairs . . .'

Ann's last words when, an hour later, they parted – Mrs and Miss Bindon Botting having returned very audibly upstairs – deserve a section to themselves.

'I wouldn't do this for every one, mind you,' whispered Ann.

H. G. Wells: *Kipps*

Captain Wentworth's letter

Mrs Croft left them, and Captain Wentworth, having sealed his letter with great rapidity, was indeed ready, and had even a hurried, agitated air, which shewed impatience to be gone. Anne knew not how to understand it. She had the kindest 'Good morning, God bless you,' from Captain Harville, but from him not a word, nor a look. He had passed out of the room without a look!

She had only time, however, to move closer to the table where he had been writing, when footsteps were heard returning; the door opened; it was himself. He begged their pardon, but he had forgotten his gloves, and instantly crossing the room to the writing table, and standing with his back towards Mrs Musgrove, he drew out a letter from under the scattered paper, placed it before Anne with eyes of glowing entreaty fixed on her for a moment, and hastily collecting his gloves, was again out of the room, almost before Mrs Musgrove was aware of his being in it – the work of an instant!

The revolution which one instant had made in Anne, was almost beyond expression. The letter, with a direction hardly legible, to 'Miss A.E. –.' was evidently the one which he had been folding so hastily. While supposed to be writing only to Captain Benwick, he had been also addressing her! On the contents of that letter depended all which this world could do for her! Any thing was possible, any thing might be defied rather than suspense. Mrs Musgrove had little arrangements of her own at her own table; to their protection she must trust, and sinking into the chair which he had occupied, succeeding to the very spot where he had leaned and written, her eyes devoured the following words:

'I can listen no longer in silence. I must speak to you by such means as are within my reach. You pierce my soul. I am half agony, half hope. Tell me not that I am too late, that such precious feelings are gone for ever. I offer myself to you again with a heart even more your own, than when you almost broke it eight years and a half ago. Dare not say that man forgets sooner than woman, that his love has an earlier death. I have loved none but you. Unjust I may have been, weak and resentful I have been, but never inconstant. You alone have brought me to Bath. For you alone I think and plan. – Have you not seen this? Can you fail to have understood my wishes? – I had not waited even these ten days, could I have read your feelings, as I think you must have penetrated mine. I can hardly write. I am every instant hearing something which overpowers me. You sink your voice, but I can distinguish the tones of that voice, when they would be lost on others. – Too good, too excellent creature! You do us justice indeed. You do believe that there is true attachment and constancy among men. Believe it to be most fervent, most undeviating in

'F.W.'

'I must go, uncertain of my fate; but I shall return hither, or follow your party, as soon as possible. A word, a look will be enough to decide whether I enter your father's house this evening, or never.'

Such a letter was not to be soon recovered from. Half an hour's solitude and reflection might have tranquillised her; but the ten minutes only, which now passed before she was interrupted, with all the restraints of her situation, could do nothing towards tranquillity. Every moment rather brought fresh agitation. It was an overpowering happiness . . .

Jane Austen: Persuasion

Shipboard romance

Scene: Deck of eastward-bound steamer. Major Dumbarton seated on deck-chair, another chair by his side, with the name 'Mrs Carewe' painted on it, a third near by.
Enter, R., Mrs Carewe, seats herself leisurely in her deckchair, the Major affecting to ignore her presence.

Reconciliations and Reunions

MAJOR [*turning suddenly*]: Emily! After all these years! This is fate!

EM.: Fate! Nothing of the sort; it's only me. You men are always such fatalists. I deferred my departure three whole weeks, in order to come out in the same boat that I saw you were travelling by. I bribed the steward to put our chairs side by side in an unfrequented corner, and I took enormous pains to be looking particularly attractive this morning, and then you say, 'This is fate.' I *am* looking particularly attractive, am I not?

MAJ.: More than ever. Time has only added a ripeness to your charms.

EM.: I knew you'd put it exactly in those words. The phraseology of love-making is awfully limited, isn't it? After all, the chief charm is in the fact of being made love to. You *are* making love to me, aren't you?

MAJ.: Emily dearest, I had already begun making advances even before you sat down here. I also bribed the steward to put our seats together in a secluded corner. 'You may consider it done, sir,' was his reply. That was immediately after breakfast.

EM.: How like a man to have his breakfast first. I attended to the seat business as soon as I left my cabin.

MAJ.: Don't be unreasonable. It was only at breakfast that I discovered your blessed presence on the boat. I paid violent and unusual attention to a flapper all through the meal in order to make you jealous. She's probably in her cabin writing reams about me to a fellow-flapper at this very moment.

EM.: You needn't have taken all that trouble to make me jealous, Dickie. You did that years ago, when you married another woman.

MAJ.: Well, you had gone and married another man – a widower, too, at that.

EM.: Well, there's no particular harm in marrying a widower, I suppose. I'm ready to do it again, if I meet a really nice one.

MAJ.: Look here, Emily, it's not fair to go at that rate. You're a lap ahead of me the whole time. It's my place to propose to you; all you've got to do is to say 'Yes.'

EM.: Well, I've practically said it already, so we needn't dawdle over that part.

MAJ.: Oh, well –

They look at each other, then suddenly embrace with considerable energy.

MAJ.: We dead-heated it that time. [*Suddenly jumping to his feet*] Oh, d— I'd forgotten!

EM.: Forgotten what?

MAJ.: The children. I ought to have told you. Do you mind children?

EM.: Not in moderate quantities. How many have you got?

MAJ.: [*counting hurriedly on his fingers*]: Five.

EM.: Five!

MAJ. [*anxiously*]: Is that too many?

EM.: It's rather a number. The worst of it is, I've some myself.

MAJ.: Many?

EM.: Eight.

MAJ.: Eight in six years! Oh, Emily!

EM.: Only four were my own. The other four were by my husband's first marriage. Still, that practically makes eight.

MAJ.: And eight and five make thirteen. We can't start our married life with thirteen children; it would be most unlucky. [*Walks up and down in agitation.*] Some way must be found out of this. If we could only bring them down to twelve. Thirteen is so horribly unlucky.

EM.: Isn't there some way by which we could part with one or two? Don't the French want more children? I've often seen articles about it in the *Figaro*.

MAJ.: I fancy they want French children. Mine don't even speak French.

EM.: There's always a chance that one of them might turn out depraved and vicious, and then you could disown him. I've heard of that being done.

MAJ.: But, good gracious, you've got to educate him first. You can't expect a boy to be vicious till he's been to a good school.

EM.: Why couldn't he be naturally depraved? Lots of boys are.

MAJ.: Only when they inherit it from depraved parents. You don't suppose there's any depravity in me, do you?

EM.: It sometimes skips a generation, you know. Weren't any of your family bad?

MAJ.: There was an aunt who was never spoken of.

EM.: There you are!

MAJ.: But one can't build too much on that. In mid-Victorian days they labelled all sorts of things as unspeakable that we should speak about quite tolerantly. I daresay this particular aunt had only married a Unitarian, or rode to hounds on both sides of her horse, or something of that sort. Anyhow, we can't wait indefinitely for one of the children to take after a doubtfully depraved great-aunt. Something else must be thought of.
EM.: Don't people ever adopt children from other families?
MAJ.: I've heard of it being done by childless couples, and those sort of people –
EM.: Hush! Some one's coming. Who is it?
MAJ.: Mrs Paly-Paget.
EM.: The very person!
MAJ.: What, to adopt a child? Hasn't she got any?
EM.: Only one miserable hen-baby.
MAJ.: Let's sound her on the subject.

Enter Mrs Paly-Paget, R.

Ah, good morning, Mrs Paly-Paget. I was just wondering at breakfast where did we meet last?
MRS P.-P.: At the Criterion, wasn't it? [*Drops into vacant chair.*]
MAJ.: At the Criterion, of course.
MRS P.-P.: I was dining with Lord and Lady Slugford. Charming people, but so mean. They took us afterwards to the Velodrome, to see some dancer interpreting Mendelssohn's 'songs without clothes.' We were all packed up in a little box near the roof, and you may imagine how hot it was. It was like a Turkish bath. And, of course, one couldn't see anything.
MAJ.: Then it was not like a Turkish bath.
MRS P.-P.: Major!
EM.: We were just talking of you when you joined us.
MRS P.-P.: Really! Nothing very dreadful, I hope.
EM.: Oh, dear, no! It's too early on the voyage for that sort of thing. We were feeling rather sorry for you.
MRS P.-P.: Sorry for me? Whatever for?
MAJ.: Your childless hearth and all that, you know. No little pattering feet.
MRS P.-P.: Major! How dare you? I've got my little girl, I suppose you know. Her feet can patter as well as other children's.

MAJ.: Only one pair of feet.

MRS P.-P.: Certainly. My child isn't a centipede. Considering the way they move us about in those horrid jungle stations, without a decent bungalow to set one's foot in, I consider I've got a heartless child, rather than a childless hearth. Thank you for your sympathy all the same. I daresay it was well meant. Impertinence often is.

EM.: Dear Mrs Paly-Paget, we were only feeling sorry for your sweet little girl when she grows older, you know. No little brothers and sisters to play with.

MRS P.-P.: Mrs Carewe, this conversation strikes me as being indelicate, to say the least of it. I've only been married two and a half years, and my family is naturally a small one.

MAJ.: Isn't it rather an exaggeration to talk of one little female child as a family? A family suggests numbers.

MRS P.-P.: Really, Major, your language is extraordinary. I daresay I've only got a little female child, as you call it, at present –

MAJ.: Oh, it won't change into a boy later on, if that's what you're counting on. Take our word for it; we've had so much more experience in these affairs than you have. Once a female, always a female. Nature is not infallible, but she always abides by her mistakes.

MRS P.-P. [*rising*]: Major Dumbarton, these boats are uncomfortably small, but I trust we shall find ample accommodation for avoiding each other's society during the rest of the voyage. The same wish applies to you, Mrs Carewe.

Exit Mrs Paly-Paget, L.

MAJ.: What an unnatural mother! [*Sinks into chair.*]

EM.: I wouldn't trust a child with any one who had a temper like hers. Oh, Dickie, why did you go and have such a large family? You always said you wanted me to be the mother of your children.

MAJ.: I wasn't going to wait while you were founding and fostering dynasties in other directions. Why you couldn't be content to have children of your own, without collecting them like batches of postage stamps, I can't think. The idea of marrying a man with four children!

EM.: Well, you're asking me to marry one with five.

MAJ.: Five! [*Springing to his feet.*] Did I say five?
EM.: You certainly said five.
MAJ.: Oh, Emily, supposing I've miscounted them! Listen now, keep count with me. Richard – that's after me, of course.
EM.: One.
MAJ.: Albert-Victor – that must have been in Coronation year.
EM.: Two!
MAJ.: Maud. She's called after –
EM.: Never mind who she's called after. Three!
MAJ.: And Gerald.
EM.: Four!
MAJ.: That's the lot.
EM.: Are you sure?
MAJ.: I swear that's the lot. I must have counted Albert-Victor as two.
EM.: Richard!
MAJ.: Emily!
They embrace.

Saki (H. H. Munro): The Baker's Dozen

No shadow of another parting

'Dear Pip,' said Biddy, 'you are sure you don't fret for her?'

'O no – I think not, Biddy.'

'Tell me as an old friend. Have you quite forgotten her?'

'My dear Biddy, I have forgotten nothing in my life that ever had a foremost place there, and little that ever had any place there. But that poor dream, as I once used to call it, has all gone by, Biddy, all gone by!'

Nevertheless, I knew while I said those words, that I secretly intended to revisit the site of the old house that evening, alone, for her sake. Yes, even so. For Estella's sake.

I had heard of her as leading a most unhappy life, and as being separated from her husband, who had used her with great cruelty, and who had become quite renowned as a compound of pride, avarice, brutality, and meanness. And I had heard of the death of her husband, from an accident consequent on his ill-treatment of a horse. This release had befallen her some two years before; for anything I knew, she was married again.

The early dinner-hour at Joe's left me abundance of time, without hurrying my talk with Biddy, to walk over to the old spot before dark. But, what with loitering on the way, to look at old objects and to think of old times, the day had quite declined when I came to the place.

There was no house now, no brewery, no building whatever left, but the wall of the old garden. The cleared space had been enclosed with a rough fence, and looking over it, I saw that some of the old ivy had struck root anew, and was growing green on low quiet mounds of ruin. A gate in the fence standing ajar, I pushed it open and went in.

A cold silvery mist had veiled the afternoon, and the moon was not yet up to scatter it. But the stars were shining beyond the mist, and the moon was coming, and the evening was not dark. I could trace out where every part of the old house had been, and where the brewery had been, and where the gates, and where the casks. I had done so, and was looking along the desolate garden-walk, when I beheld a solitary figure in it.

The figure showed itself aware of me as I advanced. It had been moving towards me, but it stood still. As I drew nearer, I saw it to be the figure of a woman. As I drew nearer yet, it was about to turn away, when it stopped, and let me come up with it. Then, it faltered as if much surprised, and uttered my name, and I cried out:

'Estella!'

'I am greatly changed. I wonder you know me.'

The freshness of her beauty was indeed gone, but its indescribable majesty and its indescribable charm remained. Those attractions in it I had seen before; what I had never seen before was the saddened softened light of the once proud eyes; what I had never felt before was the friendly touch of the once insensible hand.

We sat down on a bench that was near, and I said, 'After so many years, it is strange that we should thus meet again, Estella, here where our first meeting was! Do you often come back?'

'I have never been here since.'

'Nor I.'

The moon began to rise, and I thought of the placid look at the white ceiling, which had passed away. The moon began to rise, and I thought of the pressure on my hand when I had spoken the last words he had heard on earth.

Estella was the next to break the silence that ensued between us.

'I have very often hoped and intended to come back, but have been prevented by many circumstances. Poor, poor old place!'

The silvery mist was touched with the first rays of the moonlight, and the same rays touched the tears that dropped from her eyes. Not knowing that I saw them, and setting herself to get the better of them, she said quietly:

'Were you wondering, as you walked along, how it came to be left in this condition?'

'Yes, Estella.'

'The ground belongs to me. It is the only possession I have not relinquished. Everything else has gone from me, little by little, but I have kept this. It was the subject of the only determined resistance I made in all the wretched years.'

'Is it to be built on?'

'At last it is. I came here to take leave of it before its change. And you,' she said, in a voice of touching interest to a wanderer, 'you live abroad still.'

'Still.'

'And do well, I am sure?'

'I work pretty hard for a sufficient living, and therefore – Yes, I do well!'

'I have often thought of you,' said Estella.

'Have you?'

'Of late, very often. There was a long hard time when I kept far from me the remembrance of what I had thrown away when I was quite ignorant of its worth. But, since my duty has not been incompatible with the admission of that remembrance, I have given it a place in my heart.'

'You have always held your place in *my* heart,' I answered.

Reconciliations and Reunions

And we were silent again until she spoke.

'I little thought,' said Estella, 'that I should take leave of you in taking leave of this spot. I am very glad to do so.'

'Glad to part again, Estella? To me parting is a painful thing. To me, the remembrance of our last parting has been ever mournful and painful.'

'But you said to me,' returned Estella, very earnestly, '"God bless you, God forgive you!" And if you could say that to me then, you will not hesitate to say that to me now – now, when suffering has been stronger than all other teaching, and has taught me to understand what your heart used to be. I have been bent and broken, but – I hope – into a better shape. Be as considerate and good to me as you were, and tell me we are friends.'

'We are friends,' said I, rising and bending over her, as she rose from the bench.

'And will continue friends apart,' said Estella.

I took her hand in mine, and we went out of the ruined place; and, as the morning mists had risen long ago when I first left the forge, so, the evening mists were rising now, and in all the broad expanse of tranquil light they showed to me, I saw no shadow of another parting from her.

Charles Dickens: *Great Expectations*

Propositions

The passionate shepherd to his love

Come live with me and be my Love,
And we will all the pleasures prove
That hills and valleys, dales and fields,
Or woods or steepy mountain yields.

And we will sit upon the rocks,
And see the shepherds feed their flocks
By shallow rivers, to whose falls
Melodious birds sing madrigals.

And I will make thee beds of roses
And a thousand fragrant posies;
A cap of flowers, and a kirtle
Embroider'd all with leaves of myrtle.

A gown made of the finest wool
Which from our pretty lambs we pull;
Fair-linèd slippers for the cold,
With buckles of the purest gold.

A belt of straw and ivy-buds
With coral clasps and amber studs:
And if these pleasures may thee move,
Come live with me and be my Love.

The shepherd swains shall dance and sing
For thy delight each May morning:
If these delights thy mind may move,
Then live with me and be my Love.

                                      Christopher Marlowe

The nymph's reply

If all the world and love were young,
And truth in every shepherd's tongue,
These pretty pleasures might me move
To live with thee and be thy Love.

But Time drives flocks from field to fold;
When rivers rage and rocks grow cold;
And Philomel becometh dumb;
The rest complains of cares to come.

The flowers do fade, and wanton fields
To wayward Winter reckoning yields:
A honey tongue, a heart of gall,
Is fancy's spring, but sorrow's fall.

Thy gowns, thy shoes, thy beds of roses,
Thy cap, thy kirtle, and thy posies,
Soon break, soon wither – soon forgotten,
In folly ripe, in reason rotten.

Thy belt of straw and ivy-buds,
Thy coral clasps and amber studs, –
All these in me no means can move
To come to thee and be thy Love.

But could youth last, and love still breed,
Had joys no date, nor age no need,
Then these delights my mind might move
To live with thee and be thy Love.

Walter Raleigh

Setting out the alternatives

At the degree of intimacy which in Italy follows love, there was no longer any obstacle in the nature of vanity between the lovers. It was therefore with the most perfect simplicity that Mosca said to the woman he adored:

'I have two or three plans of conduct to offer you, all pretty well thought out; I have been thinking of nothing else for three months.

'First: I hand in my resignation, and we retire to a quiet life at Milan or Florence or Naples or wherever you please. We have an income of 15,000 francs, apart from the Prince's generosity, which will continue for some time, more or less.

'Secondly: You condescend to come to the place in which I have some authority; you buy a property, Sacca, for example, a charming house in the middle of a forest, commanding the valley of the Po; you can have the contract signed within a week from now. The Prince then attaches you to his court. But here I can see an immense objection. You will be well received at court; no one would think of refusing, with me there; besides the Princess imagines she is unhappy and I have recently rendered her certain services with an eye to your future: the Prince is a bigoted churchman, and as you know ill luck will have it that I am a married man. From which will arise a million minor unpleasantnesses. You are a widow; it is a fine title which would have to be exchanged for another, and this brings me to my third proposal.

'One might find a new husband who would not be a nuisance. But first of all he would have to be considerably advanced in years, for why should you deny me the hope of one day succeeding him? Very well, I have made this arrangement with the Duca Sanseverina-Taxis, who, of course, does not know the name of his future Duchesa. He knows only that she will make him an

Propositions

Ambassador and will procure him the Grand Cordon which his father had, and the lack of which makes him the most unhappy of mortals. Apart from this the Duca is by no means an absolute idiot; he gets his clothes from Paris. He is not in the least the sort of man who would do anything *deliberately* mean, he seriously believes that his honour consists in his having a Cordon, and he is ashamed of his riches. He came to me a year ago proposing to found a hospital, in order to get this Cordon; I laughed at him, but he did not by any means laugh at me when I made him a proposal of marriage; my first condition was, you understand, that he must never again set foot in Parma.'

'But do you know what you are proposing is highly immoral?' said the Contessa.

'No more immoral than everything else that is done at our court and a score of others. Absolute power has this advantage, that it sanctifies everything in the eyes of the public: what harm can there be in a thing that nobody notices? Our policy for the next twenty years is going to consist in fear of the Jacobins — and such fear too! Every year, we shall fancy ourselves on the eve of '93. You will hear, I hope, the fine speeches I make on the subject at my receptions! They are beautiful! Everything that can in any way reduce this fear will be *supremely moral* in the eyes of the nobles and bigots. And you see, at Parma, everyone who is not either a noble or a bigot is in prison, or is packing to go there; you may be quite sure that this marriage will not be thought odd among us until the day on which I am disgraced. This arrangement involves no dishonesty towards anyone; that is the essential thing, it seems to me. The Prince, on whose favour we are trading, has placed only one condition on his consent, which is that the future Duchesa shall be of noble birth. Last year my office, all told, brought me in 107,000 francs; my total income would therefore be 122,000; I invested 20,000 at Lyons. Very well, choose for yourself; either a life of luxury based on our having 122,000 francs to spend, which in Parma goes as far as at least 400,000 in Milan; but with this marriage which will give you the name of a passable man on whom you will never set eyes after you leave the altar; or else the simple middle-class existence of 15,000 francs at Florence or Naples, for I am of your opinion, you have been too much admired at Milan; we shall be persecuted here by envy, which might perhaps succeed in souring our tempers. Our grand life at Parma will, I hope, have some touches of novelty, even in your eyes which have seen the court of Prince Eugène; you would be wise to try it before shutting the door on it for ever. Do not think I am seeking to influence your opinion. As for me, my mind is quite made up: I would rather live on a fourth floor with you than continue that grand life by myself.'

Stendhal: *The Charterhouse of Parma*,
translated by C. K. Scott Moncrieff

Struck by the dart of love

[c. 1528]

In debating with myself the contents of your letters I have been put to a great agony; not knowing how to understand them, whether to my disadvantage as shown in some place, or to my advantage as in others. I beseech you now with all my heart definitely to let me know your whole mind as to the love between us; for necessity compels me to plague you for a reply, having been for more than a year now struck by the dart of love, and being uncertain either of failure or of finding a place in your heart and affection, which point has certainly kept me for some time from naming you my mistress, since if you only love me with an ordinary love the name is not appropriate to you, seeing that it stands for an uncommon position very remote from the ordinary; but if it pleases you to do the duty of a true, loyal mistress and friend, and to give yourself body and heart to me, who have been, and will be, your very loyal servant (if your rigour does not forbid me), I promise you that not only the name will be due to you, but also to take you as my sole mistress, casting off all others than yourself out of mind and affection, and to serve you only; begging you to make me a complete reply to this my rude letter as to how far and in what I can trust; and if it does not please you to reply in writing, to let me know of some place where I can have it by word of mouth, the which place I will seek out with all my heart. No more for fear of wearying you. Written by the hand of him who would willingly remain your

                                                         HR

Henry VIII to Anne Boleyn

Not to be forgotten

                                             6 October, 1816

You bid me to write short to you and I have much to say. You also bade me believe it was a fancy which made me cherish an attachment for you. It cannot be a fancy since you have been for the last year the object upon which every solitary moment led me to muse.

I do not expect you to love me; I am not worthy of your love. I feel you are superior – yet much to my surprise, more to my happiness, you betrayed passions I had believed no longer alive in your bosom. Shall I also have to ruefully experience the want of happiness, shall I reject it when it is offered [?]. I may appear to you imprudent, vicious, my opinions detestable, my theory depraved but one thing at least time shall show you that I love you gently and with affection, that I am incapable of anything approaching to the feeling of revenge or malice; I do assure you, your future will shall be mine and everything you shall do or say, I shall not question.

Have you then any objection to the following plan? On Thursday evening we may go out of town together by some stage or mail about the distance of 10 or 12 miles. There we shall be free and unknown; we can return early the following morning. I have arranged everything here so that the slightest suspicion may not be excited. Pray do so with your people.

Will you admit me for two minutes to settle *where*? Indeed I will not stay an instant after you tell me to go. Only so much may be said and done in a short time by an interview which writing cannot effect. Do what you will, or go where you will, refuse to see me and

Propositions

behave unkindly, I shall never forget you. I shall ever remember the gentleness of your manners and the wild originality of your countenance. Having been once seen you are not to be forgotten. Perhaps this is the last time I shall ever address you. Once more then let me assure you that I am not ungrateful. In all things have you acted most honourably, and I am only provoked that the awkwardness of my manner and something like timidity has hitherto prevented my expressing it to you personally.

> Claire Clairmont to Lord Byron

No words wasted

[*c.* 1840]
When, after seeing her act one evening, the Prince de Joinville sent Rachel his card with the famous words: 'Where? – When? – How much?' she countered:
  'Your place – Tonight – Free'.

> Antonia Fraser: *Love Letters*

Rejections and Refusals

Sarah, Duchess of Marlborough refuses the Duke of Somerset

If I were young and handsome as I was, instead of old and faded as I am, and you could lay the empire of the world at my feet, you should never share the heart and hand that once belonged to John, Duke of Marlborough.

The wrong approach

My uncle William Rosetti Mr [Henry] James considered to be an unbelievable bore. He once heard him recount how he had seen George Eliot proposed to by Herbert Spencer on the leads of the terrace at Somerset House . . .

'You would think', Mr James exclaimed with indignation, his dark eyes really flashing, 'that a man would make something out of a story like *that*. But the way he told it was like this,' and heightening and thinning his tones into a sort of querulous official organ, Mr James quoted: 'I have as a matter of fact frequently meditated on the motives which induced the Lady's refusal of one so distinguished; and after mature consideration I have arrived at the conclusion that although Mr Spencer with correctness went down upon one knee and grasped the Lady's hand he completely omitted the ceremony of removing his high hat, a proceeding which her sense of the occasion might have demanded . . .' – 'Is that', Mr James concluded, 'the way to tell *that* story?'

Ford Madox Ford: *Return to Yesterday*

Patrick Brontë and Mary Burder

[*July 28th*, 1823.]

Dear Madam,

The circumstance of Mrs Burder not answering my letter for so long a time gave me considerable uneasiness; however, I am much obliged to her for answering it at last. Owing to a letter which I received from Miss Sarah, and to my not receiving any answer to two letters which I wrote subsequently to that, I have thought for *years* past that it was highly probable you were married, or at all events, you wished to hear nothing of me, or from me, and determined that I should learn nothing of you. This not unfrequently gave me pain, but there was no remedy, and I endeavoured to resign, to what appeared to me to be the will of God.

I experienced a very agreeable sensation in my heart, at this moment, on reflecting that you are *still* single, and am so selfish as to wish you to remain so, even if you would never allow me to see you. *You* were the *first* whose hand I solicited, and no doubt I was the *first* to whom *you promised to give that hand*.

However much you may dislike me now, I am sure you once loved me with an unaffected innocent love, and I feel confident that after all which you have seen and heard you cannot doubt my love for you. This is a long interval of time and may have effected many changes. It has made me look something older. But, I trust I have gained more than I have lost, I hope I may venture to say I am wiser and better. I have found this world to be but vanity, and I trust I may aver that my heart's desire is to be found in the ways of divine Wisdom, and in her paths, which are pleasantness and peace. My dear Madam, I earnestly desire to know how it is in these respects with you. I wish, I ardently wish your *best* interests in *both* the worlds. Perhaps you have not had much trouble since I saw you, nor such experience as would unfold to your view in well-defined shapes the unsatisfactory nature of all earthly considerations. However, I trust you possess in your soul a sweet peace and serenity arising from communion with the Holy Spirit, and a well-grounded hope of eternal felicity. Though I have had much bitter sorrow in consequence of the sickness and death of my dear Wife, yet I have ample cause to praise God for his numberless mercies. I have a *small* but *sweet* little family that often soothe my heart and afford me pleasure by their endearing little ways, and I have what I consider a competency of the good things of this life. I am *now settled* in a part of the country *for life* where I have many friends, and it has pleased God in many respects to give me favour in the eyes of the people, and to prosper me in my ministerial labours. I want but *one* addition to my comforts, and then I think I should wish for no more on this side eternity. I want to see a dearly Beloved Friend, kind as I *once* saw her, and as *much* disposed to promote my happiness. If I have ever given her any pain I only wish for an opportunity to make her ample amends, by every attention and kindness. Should that very dear Friend doubt respecting the veracity of any of my statements, I would beg leave to give her the most satisfactory reference, I would beg leave to refer her to the Rev John Buckworth, Vicar of Dewsbury, near Leeds, who is an excellent and respectable man, well known both as an *Author* and an able Minister of the Gospel to the religious world.

My dear Madam, all that I have to request at present is that you will be so good as to answer this letter as soon as convenient, and tell me candidly whether you and Mrs Burder would have any objection to seeing me at Finchingfield Park as an *Old Friend*. If you would allow me to call there in a friendly manner, as soon as I could get a supply for my church and could leave home I would set off for the South. Should you object to my stopping at Finchingfield Park overnight I would stop at one of the Inns in Braintree – as most likely my old friends in that town are either dead or gone. Should you and Mrs Burder kindly consent to see me as an old friend, it might be necessary for me before I left home to write *another* letter in order that I might know when you would be at home. I cannot tell how *you* may feel on reading this, but I must say *my* ancient love is rekindled, and I have a *longing* desire to see you. Be so kind to give my best respects to Mrs Burder, to Miss Sarah, your brothers, and the *Little Baby*. And *whatever* you resolve upon, believe me to be yours *Most Sincerely*,

P. BRONTË

Finchingfield Park,
August 8th, 1823.

Reverend Sir,

As you must reasonably suppose, a letter from you presented to me on the 4th inst. naturally produced sensations of surprise and agitation. You have thought proper after a lapse of fifteen years and after various changes in circumstances again to address me, with what motives I cannot well define. The subject you have introduced, so long ago buried in silence and until now almost forgotten, cannot, I should think, produce in your mind anything like satisfactory reflection. From a recent perusal of many letters of yours bearing date eighteen hundred and eight, nine and ten addressed to myself and my dear departed Aunt, many circumstances are brought with peculiar force afresh to my recollection. With my present feelings I cannot forbear in justice to myself making some observations which may possibly appear severe – of their justice I am convinced. This review, Sir, excites in my bosom increased gratitude and thankfulness to that wise, that indulgent, Providence which then watched over me for good and withheld me from forming in very early life an indissoluble engagement with one whom I cannot think was altogether clear of duplicity. A union with you under then existing circumstances must have embittered my future days and would, I have no doubt, been productive of reflections upon me as unkind and distressing as events have proved they would have been unfounded and unjust. Happily for me I have not been the ascribed cause of hindering your promotion, of preventing any brilliant alliance, nor have those great and affluent friends that you used to write and speak of withheld their patronage on my account, young, inexperienced, unsuspecting, and ignorant as I was of what I had a right to look forward to.

Many communications were received from you in humble silence which ought rather to have met with contempt and indignation ever considering the sacredness of a promise. Your confidence I have never betrayed, strange as was the disclosure you once made unto me; whether those ardent professions of devoted lasting attachment were sincere is now to me a matter of little consequence. 'What I have seen and heard' certainly leads me to conclude very differently. With these my present views of past occurrences is it possible, think you, that I or my dear Parent could give you a cordial welcome to the Park as an *old friend*? Indeed, I must give a *decided* negative to the desired visit. I know of no ties of friendship *ever* existing between us which the last eleven or twelve years have not severed or at least placed an insuperable bar to any revival. My present condition, upon which you are pleased to remark, has hitherto been the state of my choice and to me a state of much happiness and comfort, tho' I have not been exempted from some severe trials. Blessed with the kindest and most indulgent of friends in a beloved Parent, Sister, and Brother, with a handsome competency which affords me the capability of gratifying the best feelings of my heart, teased with no domestic cares and anxieties and without anyone to control or oppose me, I have felt no willingness to risk in a change so many enjoyments in my possession. Truly I may say, 'My Cup overfloweth', yet it is ever my desire to bear mind that mutability is inscribed on all earthly possession. 'This is not my rest', and I humbly trust that I have been led to place all my hopes of present and future happiness upon a surer foundation, upon that tried foundation stone which God has laid in Zion. Within these last twelve months I have suffered a severe and protracted affliction from typhus fever. For twenty-eight weeks I was unable to leave my bedroom, and in that time was brought to the confines of an eternal world. I have indeed been brought low, but the Lord has helped me. He has been better to me than my fears, has delivered my soul from death, my eyes from tears, and my feet from falling, and I trust the grateful language of my heart is, 'What shall I render unto the Lord for all his benefits?' The life so manifestly redeemed from the grave I desire to devote more unreservedly than I have ever yet done to His service.

With the tear of unavailing sorrow still ready to start at the recollection of the loss of that beloved relative whom we have been call'd to mourn since you and I last saw each other, I can truly sympathize with you and the poor little innocents in your bereavement. The Lord can supply all your and their need. It gives me pleasure always to hear the work of the Lord prospering. May He enable you to be as faithful, as zealous, and as successful a labourer in His vineyard as was one of your predecessors, the good old Mr. Grimshaw, who occupied the pulpit at Haworth more than half a century ago, then will your consolations be neither few nor small. Cherishing no feeling of resentment or animosity, I remain, Revd Sir, sincerely your Well Wisher,

MARY D. BURDER

Tatyana and Onegin

TATYANA'S LETTER TO ONEGIN

'I write to you – no more confession
is needed, nothing's left to tell.
I know it's now in your discretion
with scorn to make my world a hell.

'But, if you've kept some faint impression
of pity for my wretched state,
you'll never leave me to my fate.
At first I thought it out of season
to speak; believe me: of my shame
you'd not so much as know the name,
if I'd possessed the slightest reason
to hope that even once a week
I might have seen you, heard you speak
on visits to us, and in greeting
I might have said a word, and then
thought, day and night, and thought again
about one thing, till our next meeting.
But you're not sociable, they say:
you find the country godforsaken;
though we . . . don't shine in any way.
our joy in you is warmly taken.

Rejections and Refusals

'Why did you visit us, but why?
Lost in our backwoods habitation
I'd not have known you, therefore I
would have been spared this laceration.
In time, who knows, the agitation
of inexperience would have passed,
I would have found a friend, another,
and in the role of virtuous mother
and faithful wife I'd have been cast.

'Another! . . . No, another never
in all the world could take my heart!
Decreed in highest court for ever . . .
heaven's will — for you I'm set apart;
and my whole life has been directed
and pledged to you, and firmly planned;
I know, Godsent one, I'm protected
until the grave by your strong hand:
you'd made appearance in my dreaming;
unseen, already you were dear,
my soul had heard your voice ring clear,
stirred at your gaze, so strange, so gleaming,
long, long ago . . . no, that could be
no dream. You'd scarce arrived, I reckoned
to know you, swooned, and in a second
all in a blaze, I said: it's he!

'You know, it's true, how I attended,
drank in your words when all was still —
helping the poor, or while I mended
with balm of prayer my torn and rended
spirit that anguish had made ill.
At this midnight of my condition,
was it not you, dear apparition,
who in the dark came flashing through
and, on my bed-head gently leaning,
with love and comfort in your meaning,

spoke words of hope? But who are you:
the guardian angel of tradition,
or some vile agent of perdition
sent to seduce? Resolve my doubt.
Oh, this could all be false and vain,
a sham that trustful souls work out;
fate could be something else again . . .

'So let it be! for you to keep
I trust my fate to your direction,
Hence forth in front of you I weep,
I weep, and pray for your protection . . .
Imagine it: quite on my own
I've no one here who comprehends me,
and now a swooning mind attends me,
dumb I must perish, and alone.
My heart awaits you: you can turn it
to life and hope with just a glance –
or else disturb my mournful trance
with censure – I've done all to earn it!

'I close. I dread to read this page . . .
for shame and fear my wits are sliding . . .
and yet your honour is my gage,
and in it boldly I'm confiding' . . .

XXXII

Now Tanya's groaning, now she's sighing;
the letter trembles in her grip;
the rosy sealing-wafer's drying
upon her feverish tongue; the slip
from off her charming shoulder's drooping,
and sideways her poor head is stooping.
But now the radiance of the moon
is dimmed. Down there the valley soon
comes clearer through the mists of dawning.
Down there, by slow degrees, the stream

has taken on a silvery gleam;
the herdsman's horn proclaimed the morning
and roused the village long ago:
to Tanya, all's an empty show.

XXXIII

She's paid the sunrise no attention,
she sits with head sunk on her breast,
over the note holds in suspension
her seal with its engraven crest.
Softly the door is opened, enter
grey Filatevna, to present her
with a small tray and a teacup.
'Get up, my child, it's time, get up!
Why, pretty one, you're up already!
My early bird! you know, last night
you gave me such a shocking fright!
but now, thank God, you're well and steady,
your night of fretting's left no trace!
fresh as a poppy-flower, your face.'

XXXIV

'Oh nurse, a favour, a petition . . .'
'Command me, darling, as you choose.'
'Now don't suppose . . . let no suspicion . . .
but, nurse, you see . . . Oh, don't refuse . . .'
'My sweet, God warrants me your debtor.'
'Then send your grandson with this letter
quickly to O . . . I mean to that . . .
the neighbour . . . you must tell the brat
that not a syllable be uttered
and not a mention of my name . . .'
'Which neighbour, dear? My head became
in these last years all mixed and fluttered.
We've many neighbours round about;
even to count them throws me out.'

Rejections and Refusals

XXXV

'How slow you are at guessing, *nyanya*!'
'My sweet, my dearest heart, I'm old,
I'm old, my mind is blunted, Tanya;
times were when I was sharp and bold:
times were, when master's least suggestion . . .'
'Oh *nyanya*, *nyanya*, I don't question . . .
what have your wits to do with me?
Now here's a letter, as you see,
addressed to Onegin' . . . 'Well, that's easy.
But don't be cross, my darling friend,
you know I'm *hard to comprehend* . . .
Why have you gone all pale and queasy?'
'It's nothing, nurse, nothing, I say . . .
just send your grandson on his way.'

XXXVI

Hours pass; no answer; waiting, waiting.
No word: another day goes by.
She's dressed since dawn, dead pale; debating,
demanding: *when* will he reply?
Olga's adorer comes a-wooing.
'Tell me, what's your companion doing?'
enquired the lady of the hall:
'it seems that he forgot us all.'
Tatyana flushed, and started shaking.
'Today he promised he'd be here,'
so Lensky answered the old dear:
'the mail explains the time he's taking.'
Tatyana lowered her regard
as at a censure that was hard.

Rejections and Refusals

XXXVII

Day faded; on the table, glowing,
the samovar of evening boiled,
and warmed the Chinese teapot; flowing
beneath it, vapour wreathed and coiled.
Already Olga's hand was gripping
the urn of perfumed tea, and tipping
into the cups its darkling stream –
meanwhile a hallboy handed cream;
before the window taking station,
plunged in reflection's deepest train,
Tatyana breathed on the cold pane,
and in the misted condensation
with charming forefinger she traced
'OE' devotedly inlaced.

XXXVIII

Meanwhile with pain her soul was girdled,
and tears were drowning her regard.
A sudden clatter! . . . blood was curdled . . .
Now nearer . . . hooves . . . and in the yard
Evgeny! 'Ah!' Tatyana, fleeting
light as a shadow, shuns a meeting,
through the back porch runs out and flies
down to the garden, and her eyes
daren't look behind her; fairly dashing –
beds, bridges, lawn, she never stops,
the *allée* to the lake, the copse;
breaking the lilac bushes, smashing
parterres, she runs to rivulet's brink,
to gasp, and on a bench to sink.

Rejections and Refusals

XXXIX

She dropped . . . 'It's he! Eugene arriving!
Oh God, what did he think!' A dream
of hope is somehow still surviving
in her torn heart – a fickle gleam;
she trembles, and with fever drumming
awaits him – hears nobody coming.
Maidservants on the beds just now
were picking berries from the bough,
singing in chorus as directed
(on orders which of course presume
that thievish mouths cannot consume
their masters' berries undetected
so long as they're employed in song:
such rustic cunning can't be wrong!) – . . .

XL

They sing; unmoved by their sweet-sounding
choruses, Tanya can but wait,
listless, impatient, for the pounding
within her bosom to abate,
and for her cheeks to cease their blushing;
but wildly still her heart is rushing,
and on her cheeks the fever stays,
more and more brightly still they blaze.
So the poor butterfly will quiver
and beat a nacreous wing when caught
by some perverse schoolboy for sport;
and so in winter-fields will shiver
the hare who from afar has seen
a marksman crouching in the green.

Rejections and Refusals

XLI

But finally she heaved a yearning
sigh, and stood up, began to pace;
she walked, but just as she was turning
into the *allée*, face to face,
she found Evgeny, eyes a-glitter,
still as a shadow, grim and bitter;
seared as by fire, she stopped. Today
I lack the strength required to say
what came from this unlooked-for meeting;
my friends, I need to pause a spell,
and walk, and breathe, before I tell
a story that still wants completing;
I need to rest from all this rhyme:
I'll end my tale some other time . . .

XII

Moments of silence, quite unbroken;
then, stepping nearer, Eugene said:
'You wrote to me, and nothing spoken
can disavow that. I have read
those words where love, without condition,
pours out its guiltless frank admission,
and your sincerity of thought
is dear to me, for it has brought
feeling to what had long been heartless;
but I won't praise you – let me join
and pay my debt in the same coin
with an avowal just as artless;
hear my confession as I stand
I leave the verdict in your hand.

Rejections and Refusals

XIII

'Could I be happy circumscribing
my life in a domestic plot;
had fortune blest me by prescribing
husband and father as my lot;
could I accept for just a minute
the homely scene, take pleasure in it –
then I'd have looked for you alone
to be the bride I'd call my own.
Without romance, or false insistence,
I'll say: with past ideals in view
I would have chosen none but you
as helpmeet in my sad existence,
as gage of all things that were good,
and been as happy . . . as I could!

XIV

'But I was simply not intended
for happiness – that alien role.
Should your perfections be expended
in vain on my unworthy soul?
Believe (as conscience is my warrant),
wedlock for us would be abhorrent.
I'd love you, but inside a day,
with custom, love would fade away;
your tears would flow – but your emotion,
your grief would fail to touch my heart,
they'd just enrage it with their dart.
What sort of roses, in your notion,
would Hymen bring us – blooms that might
last many a day, and many a night!

Rejections and Refusals

XV

'What in the world is more distressing
than households where the wife must moan
the unworthy husband through depressing
daytimes and evenings passed alone?
and where the husband, recognizing
her worth (but anathematising
his destiny) without a smile
bursts with cold envy and with bile?
For such am I. When you were speaking
to me so simply, with the fires
and force that purity inspires,
is *this* the man that you were seeking?
can it be true you must await
from cruel fortune such a fate?

XVI

'I've dreams and years past resurrection;
a soul that nothing can renew . . .
I feel a brotherly affection,
or something tenderer still, for you.
Listen to me without resentment:
girls often change to their contentment
light dreams for new ones . . . so we see
each springtime, on the growing tree,
fresh leaves . . . for such is heaven's mandate.
You'll love again, but you must teach
your heart some self-restraint; for each
and every man won't understand it
as I have . . . learn from my belief
that inexperience leads to grief.'

Rejections and Refusals

XVII

So went his sermon. Almost dying,
blinded to everything about
by mist of tears, without replying
Tatyana heard Evgeny out.
He gave his arm. In sad abstraction,
by what's called *machinal* reaction,
without a word Tatyana leant
upon it, and with head down-bent
walked homeward round the kitchen garden . . .

Alexander Pushkin: *Eugene Onegin*,
translated by Charles Johnston

Judy and Roddy

She would write him a letter, tell him all; yes, she would tell him all. Her love for him need no longer be like a half-shameful secret. If she posted a letter to-night, he would get it to-morrow morning, just before he left.

She wrote:

Roddy, this is to say good-bye once more and to send you all my love till we meet again. I do love you, indeed, in every sort of way, and to any degree you can possibly imagine; and beyond that more, more, more, unimaginably. The more my love for you annihilates me, the more it becomes a sense of inexhaustible power.

Do you love me, Roddy? Tell me again that you do; and don't think me importunate.

I am so wrapped round and rich in my thoughts of you that at the moment I feel I can endure your absence. I almost welcome it because it will give me time to sit alone, and begin to realise my happiness. So that when you come back – Oh Roddy, come back soon!

I have loved you ever since I first saw you when we were little, I suppose, – only you, always you. I'm not likely ever to stop loving you. Thank God I can tell you so at last. Will you go on loving me? Am I to go on loving you? Oh but you won't say no, after last night. If you don't want to be tied quite yet, I shall understand. I can wait years quite happily, if you love me. Roddy I am yours. Last night I gave you what has always belonged to you. But I can't think about last night yet. It is too close and tremendous and shattering. I gasp and nearly faint when I try to recall it. I dissolve.

When I came back to my room in the dawn I stared and stared at my face in the glass, wondering how it was I could recognise it. How is it I look the same, and move, eat, speak, much as usual?

Ought I to have been more coy, more reluctant last night? Would it have been more fitting – would you have respected me more? Was I too bold? Oh, this is foolishness: I had no will but yours. But because I love you so much I am a little fearful. So write to me quickly and tell me what to think, feel, do. I shall dream till then.

There is so much more to tell you, and yet it is all the same really. My darling, I love you!

Judy.

She posted it. Next morning she hurriedly dressed and ran downstairs in the sudden expectation of finding a letter from him; but there was none.

Now he would have got hers . . . Now he would have read it . . . Now he would be walking to the station . . .

Perhaps Roddy had written her a letter just before he had gone away; and if so it might have come by the evening post. She left the river and went to seek it.

Who could it be coming towards her down the little pathway which led from the station to the bottom of the garden and then on to the blue gate in the wall of the garden next door? She stood still under the overhanging lilacs and may-trees, her heart pounding, her limbs melting. It was Roddy, in a white shirt and white flannels,

– coming from the station. He caught sight of her, seemed to hesitate, came on till he was close to her; and she had the strangest feeling that he intended to pass right by her as if he did not see her . . . What was the word for his face? Smooth: yes, smooth as a stone. She had never before noticed what a smooth face he had; but she could not see him clearly because of the beating of her pulses.

'Roddy!'

He lifted his eyebrows.

'Oh, hullo, Judith.'

'I thought you'd gone away.'

'I'm going to-morrow. A girl I know rang up this morning to suggest coming down for the day, so I waited. I've just seen her off.'

A girl he knew . . . Roddy had always had this curious facility in the dealing of verbal wounds.

'I see . . . How nice.'

A face smooth and cold as a stone. Not the faintest expression in it. Had he bidden the girl he knew good-bye with a face like this? No, it had certainly been twinkling and teasing then.

'Well I must get on.' He looked up the path as if meditating immediate escape; then said, without looking at her, and in a frozen voice: 'I got a letter from you this morning.'

'Oh you did get it?'

There could never have been a more foolish-sounding bleat. In the ensuing silence she added feebly: 'Shall you – answer it – some time?'

'I thought the best thing I could do was to leave it unanswered.'

'Oh . . .'

Because of course it had been so improper, so altogether monstrous to write like that . . .

'Well', she said. 'I thought . . . I'm sorry.'

She ought to apologise to him, because he had meant to go away without saying anything, and she had come on him unawares and spoilt his escape.

'I was very much surprised at the way you wrote', he said.

'How do you mean, surprised, Roddy?' she said timidly.

She had known all along in the deepest layer of her consciousness that something like this would happen. Permanent happiness had never been for her.

It was not much of a shock. In a moment that night was a far, unreal memory.

'Well' – he hesitated. 'If a man wants to ask a girl to – marry him he generally asks her himself – do you see?'

'You mean – it was outrageous of me not to wait – to write like that?'

I thought it a little odd.'

'Oh, but Roddy, surely – surely that's one of those worn-out conventions . . . Surely a woman has a perfect right to say she – loves a man – if she wants to – it's simply a question of having the courage . . . I can't see why not . . . I've always believed one should . . .'

It was no good trying to expostulate, to bluff like that, with his dead face confronting her. He would not be taken in by any such lying gallantries. How did one combat people whose features never gave way by so much as a quiver? She leaned against the wooden fence and tried to fix her eyes upon the may-tree opposite. Very far, but clear, she heard her mother at the other end of the garden, calling her name: but that was another Judith.

'I'm afraid you've misunderstood me', he said.

Rosamond Lehmann: *Dusty Answer*

Breach of Promise

Complications

Dr Smart-Allick and his love were talking in the rose garden at St Ethelfrith's. The air was still, the moon was full.

'Tell me, Smarty, have there been other women in your life?'

'Delicate water-lily, I cannot lie to you.'

'Well?'

'I would rather keep silent, my dainty bird of Paradise, upon so weighty a matter.'

'But – but you haven't ever actually been married?'

'Sweet morsel, enchanting may-bud, in his time a man plays many parts. If I have now and then lent the glamour of my name to this or that member of your delightful sex, 'twas but a passing whim, naught but a passing whim, devastating lodestar.'

'Oh, you are false, false, false! Where are they now?'

'Seven in gaol, two at large under assumed names, one on the run, one in Australia,' replied the Doctor briskly, ticking them off on his fingers.

Topsy wept softly.

So strong, however, is the call of love that the Doctor and Topsy met again the next night in the rose-garden at St Ethelfrith's.

'No, no. Come no nearer, heartless Lothario that you are.'

'Exquisite bud of May, can you not let bygones be bygones – including that provocative widow from Hunstanton?'

'Oh, Smarty, how can I know that you will not, even when we are one, desert me for some more exotic blossom?'

'When we are one? What can my delicious baggage mean by that?'

'Why, when we are married, my cruel Adonis.'

'What have I ever said, ineffable distraction, that would lead you to believe me capable of offering such a base insult to one so like the driven snow? I, who am smirched with a myriad conquests, dare scarcely raise my dazzled eyes to the blazing sun of your beauty and goodness. And you speak of marriage!'

'I understood that our troth was plighted.'

'Plighted my foot, my old cockyolly bird! There must be some mistake.'

The voices ceased. The Doctor strode from the garden. In his heart a bell tolled, and he heard on the breeze a fairy melody which said, 'Suppose she starts the breach of promise racket?'

The forlorn Topsy gazed disconsolately at the moon, and wondered how much money it takes to mend the heart of a fond and foolish headmistress.

On yet another night they met in the rose-arbour.

'Devastating lodestar, I am sure you understand that I have too much decency ever to ask you to become engaged to me with all these so-called Mrs Smart-Allicks round the place.'

'Heartless Don Juan, do you think a girl such as I would have consented to meet you without a chaperon, had she not believed your intentions to be honourable?'

'But, tiresome enchantress, you have no proof that I ever proposed marriage to you.'

'None, false one. I destroyed all your letters, as you bade me.'

'Excellent morsel! Entrancing elf! Thoughtful witch!'

'But stay, there was that telephone conversation which was overheard by my head monitor Agnes Hauticourt.'

'Thunder and lightning! How could she have overheard it?'

'There's an extension in the monitors' Common Room.'

'Triple damnation! Intoxicating viper, what have you done?'

The Doctor strode from the garden, his strong features working nervously.

Topsy smiled in the darkness.

Beachcomber (J. B. Morton): Dr Smart-Allick at Narkover

mehitabel has an adventure

back to the city archy
and dam glad of it
there s something about the suburbs
that gets on a town lady s nerves
fat slick tabbies
sitting around those country clubs
and lapping up the cream
of existence
none of that for me
give me the alley archy
me for the mews and the roofs
of the city
an occasional fish head
and liberty is all i ask
freedom and the garbage can
romance archy romance is the word
maybe i do starve sometimes
but wotthehell archy wotthehell
i live my own life
i met a slick looking tom
out at one of these long island
spotless towns
he fell for me hard
he slipped me into the
pantry and just as we had got
the ice-box door open and were
about to sample the cream
in comes his mistress
why fluffy she says to this slicker

Breach of Promise

the idea of you making
friends with a horrid creature like that
and what did fluffy do
stand up for me like a gentleman
make good on all the promises
with which he had lured me
into his house
not he the dirty slob
he pretended he did not know me
he turned upon me and attacked me
to make good with his boss
you mush faced bum i said
and clawed a piece out of his ear
i am a lady archy
always a lady
but an aristocrat will always
resent an insult
the woman picked up a mop and made
for me well well madam i said
it is unfortunate for you that
you have on sheer silk stockings
and i wrote my protest
on her shin it took reinforcements
in the shape of the cook
to rauss me archy and as i went
out the window i said to the fluffy person
you will hear from me later
he had promised me everything archy
that cat had
he had practically abducted me
and then the cheap crook threw me down
before his swell friends
no lady loves a scene archy
and i am always the lady no matter
what temporary disadvantages
i may struggle under
to hell with anything unrefined
has always been my motto

Breach of Promise

violence archy always does something
to my nerves
but an aristocrat must revenge
an insult i owe it to my family
to protect my good name
so i laid for that slob
for two days and nights and finally
i caught the boob in the shrubbery
pretty thing i said
it hurts me worse than it does you
to remove that left eye of yours
but i did it with one sweep of my claws
you call yourself a gentleman do you
i said as i took a strip out of his nose
you will think twice after this before
you offer an insult
to an unprotected young tabby
where is the little love nest you spoke
of i asked him
you go and lie down there i said
and maybe you can incubate another ear
because i am going to take one of yours right off now
and with those words i made ribbons
out of it you are the guy
i said to him that was going to give
me an easy life sheltered from all
the rough ways of the world
fluffy dear you don t know what the
rough ways of the world are
and i am going to show you
i have got you out here
in the great open spaces
where cats are cats
and im gonna make you understand
the affections of a lady ain t to be
trifled with by any slicker like you
where is that red ribbon with the
silver bells you promised me

Breach of Promise

the next time you betray the trust
of an innocent female
reflect on whether she may
carry a wallop little fiddle strings
this is just a mild lesson i am giving
you tonight i said as i took
the fur off his back and you oughta
be glad you didn't make me really
angry my sense of dignity is all that
saves you a lady little sweetness
never loses her poise and i thank god
i am always a lady even if i do
live my own life and with that i
picked him up by what was left of
his neck like a kitten and laid him
on the doormat slumber gently and
sweet dreams fluffy dear i said and
when you get well make it a rule of
your life never to trifle with another
girlish confidence i have been
abducted again and again by a dam
sight better cats than he ever was
or will be
well archy the world is full of ups
and downs but toujours gai is my motto
cheerio my deario
                                      archy

Don Marquis: *archy and mehitabel*

Happy

Endings

Pulling together

They had been floating about all the morning, from gloomy St Gingolf to sunny Montreux, with the Alps of Savoy on one side, Mont St Bernard and the Dent du Midi on the other, pretty Vevay in the valley, and Lausanne upon the hill beyond, a cloudless blue sky overhead, and the bluer lake below, dotted with the picturesque boats that look like white-winged gulls.

They had been talking of Bonnivard, as they glided past Chillon, and of Rousseau, as they looked up at Clarens, where he wrote his 'Héloise.' Neither had read it, but they knew it was a love-story, and each privately wondered if it was half as interesting as their own. Amy had been dabbling her hand in the water during the little pause that fell between them, and, when she looked up, Laurie was leaning on his oars, with an expression in his eyes that made her say hastily, merely for the sake of saying something, –

'You must be tired; rest a little, and let me row; it will do me good; for, since you came, I have been altogether lazy and luxurious.'

'I'm not tired; but you may take an oar, if you like. There's room enough, though I have to sit nearly in the middle, else the boat won't trim,' returned Laurie, as if he rather liked the arrangement.

Feeling that she had not mended matters much, Amy took the offered third of a seat, shook her hair over her face, and accepted an oar. She rowed as well as she did many other things; and, though she used both hands, and Laurie but one, the oars kept time, and the boat went smoothly through the water.

'How well we pull together, don't we?' said Amy, who objected to silence just then.

'So well that I wish we might always pull in the same boat. Will you, Amy?' very tenderly.

'Yes, Laurie,' very low.

Then they both stopped rowing, and unconsciously added a pretty little *tableau* of human love and happiness to the dissolving views reflected in the lake.

Louisa M. Alcott: Good Wives

A business arrangement

No one ever knew why Mr Lennox did not keep to his appointment on the following day. Mr Thornton came true to his time; and, after keeping him waiting for nearly an hour, Margaret came in looking very white and anxious.

She began hurriedly:

'I am so sorry Mr Lennox is not here, – he could have done it so much better than I can. He is my adviser in this –'

'I am sorry that I came, if it troubles you. Shall I go to Mr Lennox's chambers and try and find him?'

'No, thank you. I wanted to tell you, how grieved I was to find that I am to lose you as a tenant. But Mr Lennox says, things are sure to brighten –'

'Mr Lennox knows little about it,' said Mr Thornton quietly. 'Happy and fortunate in all a man cares for, he does not understand what it is to find oneself no longer young – yet thrown back to the starting-point which requires the hopeful energy of youth – to feel one half of life gone, and nothing done – nothing remaining of wasted opportunity, but the bitter recollection that it has been. Miss Hale, I would rather not hear Mr Lennox's opinion of my affairs. Those who are happy and successful themselves are too apt to make light of the misfortunes of others.'

'You are unjust,' said Margaret, gently. 'Mr Lennox has only spoken of the great probability which he believes there to be of your redeeming – your more than redeeming – what you have lost. Don't speak till I have ended – pray don't!' And collecting herself once more, she went on rapidly turning over some law papers, and statements of accounts in a trembling hurried manner. 'Oh! here it is! and – he drew me out a proposal – I wish he was here to explain it – showing that if you would take some money of mine, eighteen thousand and fifty-seven pounds, lying just at this moment unused in the bank, and bringing me in only two and a half per cent – you could pay me much better interest, and might go on working Marlborough Mills.' Her voice had cleared itself and become more steady. Mr Thornton did not speak, and she went on looking for some paper on which were written down the proposals for security; for she was most anxious to have it all looked upon in the light of a mere business arrangement, in which the principal advantage would be on her side. While she sought for this paper, her very heart-pulse was arrested by the tone in which Mr Thornton spoke. His voice was hoarse, and trembling with tender passion, as he said:

'Margaret!'

For an instant she looked up; and then sought to veil her luminous eyes by dropping her forehead on her hands. Again, stepping nearer, he besought her with another tremulous eager call upon her name.

'Margaret!'

Still lower went the head: more closely hidden was the face, almost resting on the table before her. He came close to her. He knelt by her side, to bring his face to a level with her ear; and whispered – panted out the words:

'Take care. – If you do not speak – I shall claim you as my own in some strange presumptuous way. – Send me away at once, if I must go; – Margaret! –'

At that third call she turned her face, still covered with her small white hands, towards him, and laid it on his shoulder, hiding it even there; and it was too delicious to feel her soft cheek against his, for him to wish to see either deep blushes or loving eyes. He clasped her close. But they both kept silence. At length she murmured in a broken voice:

'Oh, Mr Thornton, I am not good enough!'

'Not good enough! Don't mock my own deep feeling of unworthiness.'

After a minute or two, he gently disengaged her hands from her face, and laid her arms as they had once before been placed to protect him from the rioters.

'Do you remember, love?' he murmured. 'And how I requited you with my insolence the next day?'

'I remember how wrongly I spoke to you, – that is all.'

'Look here! Lift up your head. I have something to show you!' She slowly faced him, glowing with beautiful shame.

'Do you know these roses?' he said, drawing out his pocketbook, in which were treasured up some dead flowers.

'No!' she replied, with innocent curiosity. 'Did I give them to you?'

'No! Vanity; you did not. You may have worn sister roses very probably.'

She looked at them, wondering for a minute, then she smiled a little as she said –

'They are from Helstone, are they not? I know the deep indentations round the leaves. Oh! have you been there? When were you there?'

'I wanted to see the place where Margaret grew to what she is, even at the worst time of all, when I had no hope of ever calling her mine. I went there on my return from Havre.'

'You must give them to me,' she said, trying to take them out of his hand with gentle violence.

'Very well. Only you must pay me for them!'

'How shall I ever tell aunt Shaw?' she whispered, after some time of delicious silence.

'Let me speak to her.'

'Oh, no! I owe to her, – but what will she say?'

'I can guess. Her first exclamation will be, "That man!"'

'Hush!' said Margaret, 'or I shall try and show you your mother's indignant tones as she says, "That woman!"'

Elizabeth Gaskell: *North and South*

Among the primroses

At that moment Colette emerged from the lane and turned towards the village ahead of him, walking slowly and not noticing him. Henry walked for a while quietly behind her at a distance of about twenty yards. The road was straight here, bordered on one side by the elders and on the other by a wide grassy verge and a line of elm trees. Among the elders and the foot of the trees a great many primroses were still in flower. Henry's catlike footsteps were silent. The westering sun laid his long shadow down before him. He now increased his pace until his shadow head reached Colette and then passed her. Seeing the shadow at her feet Colette turned round, then stopped. Henry too stopped instantly and stared at her in silence.

'Oh – hello, Henry.'

She was wearing the green knee breeches which she had had on when she had spoken to Henry and Stephanie in the Volvo, only now instead of the tweed jacket she was wearing a light brown Russian style shirt open at the neck. Her sea-brown hair was piled up behind her head, cunningly rolled under and pinned. She was carrying a basket. The bandage had been removed from her cheek revealing a long livid furrow.

'Hello,' said Henry. But he stood still.

Colette, who had not smiled, stared at him for a moment. Then when he did not speak she gave a vague wave of her hand and turned and walked on. Henry began to walk too, padding about ten yards behind her. A car passed them.

Colette stopped again and turned, stepping on to the grass verge. Henry stopped too, not yet near her. She looked at him frowning.

'What's the matter?'

Henry advanced a pace or two in the long grass. 'Where are you going?'

Happy Endings

'To the village.'

'What for?'

'To get some beer and tobacco for Daddy.'

As Henry said nothing she began uncertainly to turn away.

'Wait a moment,' said Henry. He stepped through the grass until he stood before her. 'Colette, listen. Last time I met you wearing those totally absurd but I must say rather fetching trousers you told me that you loved me. Later on you denied this proposition. I find it hard to believe however that you really changed your mind. Your first statement carried conviction, your second did not. Do you, please, still love me?'

Collette looked at him, narrowing her eyes against the sun. Then she threw her basket sideways into the grass. 'Yes, of course, I still love you.'

'In that case,' said Henry, 'we shall get married, because I love you too – Colette –'

'Don't you mind – my face?'

'Oh *God*,' said Henry, 'you *idiot!*' He took another step and fell on his knees at her feet in the long grass. As he stretched out his arms to the green breeches and the embroidered hem of the brown shirt she subsided towards him and he took her swaying shoulders and keeled over with her among the primroses. 'Colette – forgive me – this is true, isn't it – this is it – you do love me, don't you? I know I don't deserve it – but I couldn't bear it if you didn't any more, I should die and you'd have to shovel me into the ditch.'

'I do love you, oh Henry, I've cried so about you, I thought I'd lost you – I only said I didn't love you because – you know – what was the use – and I wished so much I hadn't said that stupid thing about wanting the Hall, I don't care about anything, I don't want anything, except you, I'll go with you anywhere, I don't mind how poor we are –'

'You don't rate my earning capacity very highly,' said Henry, holding her rigidly and looking into her face, his head pillowed on her arm.

'I'll go away with you anywhere –'

'Whither I go thou wilt go and my people shall be thy people and my God thy God?'

'Yes, yes, yes.'

Happy Endings

'And you don't want to marry that bloody man Giles Gosling?'
'No! But what about –?'
'I'll tell you about that later,' said Henry. 'I'll tell you about everything later, everything that I know, and you shall explain me to myself. I shall empty myself and your grace and your truth will fill me. May I kiss you?'
'Yes, Henry.'
He pulled her closer and kissed her, gently, carefully.
'Your lips taste of apples.'
'Oh Henry, I love you so much, I'm so happy –'
'This grass is bloody wet,' said Henry. 'I suppose it's the dew. Is it the dew?'

Iris Murdoch: Henry and Cato

Spelling it out

Shtcherbatsky moved away from them, and Kitty, going up to a card-table, sat down, and, taking up the chalk, began drawing diverging circles over the new green cloth.

They began again on the subject that had been started at dinner – the liberty and occupations of women. Levin was of the opinion of Darya Alexandrovna that a girl who did not marry should find a woman's duties in a family. He supported this view by the fact that no family can get on without women to help; that in every family, poor or rich, there are and must be nurses, either relations or hired.

'No,' said Kitty, blushing, but looking at him all the more boldly with her truthful eyes; 'a girl may be so circumstanced that she cannot live in the family without humiliation, while she herself . . .'

At the hint he understood her.
'Oh yes,' he said. 'Yes, yes, yes – you're right; you're right!'
And he saw all that Pestsov had been maintaining at dinner of the liberty of woman, simply from getting a glimpse of the terror of an

Happy Endings

old maid's existence and its humiliation in Kitty's heart; and loving her, he felt that terror and humiliation, and at once gave up his arguments.

A silence followed. She was still drawing with the chalk on the table. Her eyes were shining with a soft light. Under the influence of her mood he felt in all his being a continually growing tension of happiness.

'Ah! I've scribbled all over the table!' she said, and, laying down the chalk, she made a movement as though to get up.

'What! shall I be left alone – without her?' he thought with horror, and he took the chalk. 'Wait a minute,' he said, sitting down to the table. 'I've long wanted to ask you one thing.'

He looked straight into her caressing, though frightened eyes.

'Please, ask it.'

'Here,' he said; and he wrote the initial letters, $w, y, t, m, i, c, n, b, d, t, m, n, o, t$. These letters meant, 'When you told me it could never be, did that mean never, or then?' There seemed no likelihood that she could make out this complicated sentence; but he looked at her as though his life depended on her understanding the words. She glanced at him seriously, then leaned her puckered brow on her hands and began to read. Once or twice she stole a look at him, as though asking him, 'Is it what I think?'

'I understand,' she said, flushing a little.

'What is this word?' he said, pointing to the n that stood for *never*.

'It means *never*,' she said; 'but that's not true!'

He quickly rubbed out what he had written, gave her the chalk, and stood up. She wrote, t, i, c, n, a, d.

Dolly was completely comforted in the depression caused by her conversation with Alexey Alexandrovitch when she caught sight of the two figures: Kitty with the chalk in her hand, with a shy and happy smile looking upwards at Levin, and his handsome figure bending over the table with glowing eyes fastened one minute on the table and the next on her. He was suddenly radiant: he had understood. It meant, 'Then I could not answer differently.'

He glanced at her questioningly, timidly.

'Only then?'

'Yes,' her smile answered.

'And n . . . and now?' he asked.

'Well, read this. I'll tell you what I should like – should like so much!' She wrote the initial letters, *i, y, c, f, a, f, w, h*. This meant, 'If you could forget and forgive what happened.'

He snatched the chalk with nervous, trembling fingers, and, breaking it, wrote the initial letters of the following phrase, 'I have nothing to forget and to forgive; I have never ceased to love you.'

She glanced at him with a smile that did not waver.

'I understand,' she said in a whisper.

He sat down and wrote a long phrase. She understood it all, and without asking him, 'Is it this?' took the chalk and at once answered.

For a long while he could not understand what she had written, and often looked into her eyes. He was stupefied with happiness. He could not supply the words she had meant; but in her charming eyes, beaming with happiness, he saw all he needed to know. And he wrote three letters. But he had hardly finished writing when she read them over her arm, and herself finished and wrote the answer, 'Yes.'

'You're playing secrétaire?' said the old prince. 'But we must really be getting along if you want to be in time at the theatre.'

Levin got up and escorted Kitty to the door.

In their conversation everything had been said; it had been said that she loved him, and that she would tell her father and mother that he would come to-morrow morning.

Leo Tolstoy: *Anna Karenina*, translated
by Constance Garnett

Love on the hunting-field

After running about three-quarters of a mile at best pace, Mr Sponge viewed the fox crossing a large grass field with all the steam up he could raise, a few hundred yards a-head of the pack, who were streaming along most beautifully, not viewing, but gradually

Happy Endings

gaining upon him. At last they broke from scent to view, and presently rolled him over and over among them.

'WHO-HOOP!' screamed Mr Sponge, throwing himself off his horse and rushing in amongst them. 'WHO-HOOP!' repeated he, still louder, holding the fox up in grim death above the baying pack.

'*Who-hoop!*' exclaimed Miss Glitters, reining up in delight alongside the chestnut. '*Who-hoop!*' repeated she, diving into the saddle-pocket for her lace-fringed handkerchief.

'Throw me my whip!' cried Mr Sponge, repelling the attacks of the hounds from behind with his heels. Having got it, he threw the fox on the ground, and clearing a circle, he off with his brush in an instant. 'Tear him and eat him!' cried he, as the pack broke in on the carcass. 'Tear him and eat him!' repeated he, as he made his way up to Miss Glitters with the brush, exclaiming, 'We'll put this in your hat, alongside the cock's feathers.'

The fair lady leant towards him, and as he adjusted it becomingly in her hat, looking at her bewitching eyes, her lovely face, and feeling the sweet fragrance of her breath, a something shot through Mr Sponge's pull-devil, pull-baker coat, his corduroy waistcoat, his Eureka shirt, Angola vest, and penetrated the very cockles of his heart. He gave her such a series of smacking kisses as startled her horse and astonished a poacher who happened to be hid in the adjoining hedge.

Sponge was never so happy in his life. He could have stood on his head, or been guilty of any sort of extravagance, short of wasting his money. Oh, he was happy! Oh, he was joyous! He was intoxicated with pleasure. As he eyed his angelic charmer, her lustrous eyes, her glowing cheeks, her pearly teeth, the bewitching fulness of her elegant *tournure*, and thought of the masterly way she rode the run – above all, of the dashing style in which she charged the mill-race – he felt a something quite different to anything he had experienced with any of the buxom widows or lackadaisical misses whom he could just love or not, according to circumstances, among whom his previous experience had lain. Miss Glitters, he knew, had nothing, and yet he felt he could not do without her; the puzzlement of his mind was, how the deuce they should manage matters – 'make tongue and buckle meet,' as he elegantly phrased it.

Happy Endings

It is pleasant to hear a bachelor's *pros* and *cons* on the subject of matrimony; how the difficulties of the gentleman out of love vanish or change into advantages with the one in – 'Oh, I would never think of marrying without a couple of thousand a year at the *very least*' exclaims young Fastly. '*I* can't do without four hunters and a hack. *I* can't do without a valet. *I* can't do without a brougham. *I* must belong to half-a-dozen clubs. *I'll* not marry any woman who can't keep me comfortable – bachelors can live upon nothing – bachelors are welcome everywhere – very different thing with a wife. Frightful things milliners' bills – fifty guineas for a dress, twenty for a bonnet – ladies' maids are the very devil – never satisfied – far worse to please than their mistresses.' And between the whiffs of a cigar he hums the old saw,

> Needles and pins, needles and pins,
> When a man marries his sorrow begins.

Now take him on the other tack – Fast is smitten.

'Ord hang it! a married man can live on very little,' soliloquises our friend. 'A nice lovely creature to keep one at home. Hunting's all humbug; it's only the flash of the thing that makes one follow it. Then the danger far more than counterbalances the pleasure. Awful places one has to ride over, to be sure, or submit to be called 'slow'. Horrible thing to set up for a horseman, and then have to ride to maintain one's reputation. Will be thankful to give it up altogether. The bays will make capital carriage-horses, and one can often pick up a second-hand carriage as good as new. Shall save no end of money by not having to put 'B' to my name in the assessed tax-paper. One club's as good as a dozen – will give up the Polyanthus and the Sunflower, and the Refuse and the Rag. Ladies' dresses are cheap enough. Saw a beautiful gown t'other day for a guinea. Will start Master Bergamotte. Does nothing for his wages; will scarce clean my boots. Can get a chap for half what I give him, who'll do double the work. Will make Beans into coachman. What a convenience to have one's wife's maid to sew on one's buttons, and keep one's toes in one's stocking-feet! Declare I lose half my things at the washing for want of marking. Hanged if I won't marry and be respectable – marriage is an honourable state!' And thereupon Tom grows a couple of inches taller in his own conceit.

Happy Endings

Though Mr Sponge's thoughts did not travel in quite such a luxurious first-class train as the foregoing, he, Mr Sponge, being more of a two-shirts-and-a-dicky sort of man, yet still the future ways and means weighed upon his mind, and calmed the transports of his present joy. Lucy was an angel! about that there was no dispute. He would make her Mrs Sponge at all events. Touring about was very expensive. He could only counterbalance the extravagance of inns by the rigid rule of giving nothing to servants at private houses. He thought a nice airy lodging in the suburbs of London would answer every purpose, while his accurate knowledge of cab-fares would enable Lucy to continue her engagement at the Royal Amphitheatre without incurring the serious overcharges the inexperienced are exposed to. 'Where one can dine, two can dine,' mused Mr Sponge; 'and I make no doubt we'll manage matters somehow.'

'Twopence for your thoughts!' cried Lucy, trotting up, and touching him gently on the back with her light silver-mounted riding-whip. 'Twopence for your thoughts!' repeated she, as Mr Sponge sauntered leisurely along, regardless of the bitter cold, followed by such of the hounds as chose to accompany him.

'Oh!' replied he, brightening up; 'I was just thinking what a deuced good run we'd had.'

'*Indeed!*' pouted the fair lady.

'No, my darling; I was thinking what a very pretty girl you are,' rejoined he sidling his horse up, and encircling her neat waist with his arm.

A sweet smile dimpled her plump cheeks, and chased the recollection of the former answer away.

It would not be pretty – indeed, we could not pretend to give even the outline of the conversation that followed. It was carried on in such broken and disjointed sentences, eyes and squeezes doing so much more work than words, that even a reporter would have had to draw largely upon his imagination for the substance. Suffice it to say, that though the thermometer was below zero, they never moved out of a foot's pace; the very hounds growing tired of the trail, and slinking off one by one as opportunity occurred.

A dazzling sun was going down with a blood-red glare, and the partially softened ground was fast resuming its fretwork of frost, as our hero and heroine were seen sauntering up the western avenue to Nonsuch House, as slowly and quietly as if it had been the hottest evening in summer.

'Here's old Coppertops!' exclaimed Captain Seedeybuck, as, turning round in the billiard-room to chalk his cue, he espied them crawling along. 'And Lucy!' added he, as he stood watching them.

'How slow they come!' observed Bob Spangles, going to the window.

'Must have tired their horses,' suggested Captain Quod.

'Just the sort of man to tire a horse,' rejoined Bob Spangles.

'Hate that Sponge,' observed Captain Cutitfat.

'So do I,' replied Captain Quod.

'Well, never mind the beggar! It's you to play!' exclaimed Bob Spangles to Captain Seedeybuck.

But Lady Scattercash, who was observing our friends from her boudoir window, saw with a woman's eye that there was something more than a mere case of tired horses; and, tripping down stairs she arrived at the front door just as the fair Lucy dropped smilingly from her horse into Mr Sponge's extended arms. Hurrying up into the boudoir, Lucy gave her ladyship one of Mr Sponge's modified kisses, revealing the truth more eloquently than words could convey.

R. S. Surtees: *Mr Sponge's Sporting Tour*

The simplest pattern

He had arranged to meet Sally on Saturday in the National Gallery. She was to come there as soon as she was released from the shop and had agreed to lunch with him. Two days had passed since he had seen her, and his exultation had not left him for a moment. It was because he rejoiced in the feeling that he had not attempted to see her. He had repeated to himself exactly what he would say to her and how he should say it. Now his impatience was unbearable. He had written to Doctor South and had in his pocket a telegram from him received that morning: *'Sacking the mumpish fool. When will you come?'*

He thought of Sally, with her kind blue eyes; and his lips unconsciously formed themselves into a smile. He walked up the steps of the National Gallery and sat down in the first room, so that he should see her the moment she came in. It always comforted him to get among pictures. He looked at none in particular, but allowed the magnificence of their colour, the beauty of their lines, to work upon his soul. His imagination was busy with Sally. It would be pleasant to take her away from that London in which she seemed an unusual figure, like a cornflower in a shop among orchids and azaleas; he had learned in the Kentish hop-field that she did not belong to the town; and he was sure that she would blossom under the soft skies of Dorset to a rarer beauty. She came in, and he got up to meet her. She was in black, with white cuffs at her wrists and a lawn collar round her neck. They shook hands.

'Have you been waiting long?'

'No. Ten minutes. Are you hungry?'

'Not very.'

'Let's sit here for a bit, shall we?'

'If you like.'

They sat quietly, side by side, without speaking. Philip enjoyed having her near him. He was warmed by her radiant health. A glow of life seemed like an aureole to shine about her.

'Well, how have you been?' he said at last, with a little smile.

'Oh, it's all right. It was a false alarm.'

'Was it?'

'Aren't you glad?'

An extraordinary sensation filled him. He had felt certain that Sally's suspicion was well-founded; it had never occurred to him for an instant that there was a possibility of error. All his plans were suddenly overthrown, and the existence, so elaborately pictured, was no more than a dream which would never be realised. He was free once more. Free! He need give up none of his projects, and life still was in his hands for him to do what he liked with. He felt no exhilaration, but only dismay. His heart sank. The future stretched out before him in desolate emptiness. It was as though he had sailed for many years over a great waste of waters, with peril and privation, and at last had come upon a fair haven, but as he was about to enter, some contrary wind had arisen and drove him out again into the open sea; and because he had let his mind dwell on these soft meads and pleasant woods of the land, the vast deserts of the ocean filled him with anguish. He could not confront again the loneliness and the tempest. Sally looked at him with her clear eyes.

'Aren't you glad?' she asked again. 'I thought you'd be as pleased as Punch.'

He met her gaze haggardly. 'I'm not sure,' he muttered.

'You are funny. Most men would.'

He realised that he had deceived himself; it was no self-sacrifice that had driven him to think of marrying, but the desire for a wife and a home and love; and now that it all seemed to slip through his fingers he was seized with despair. He wanted all that more than anything in the world. What did he care for Spain and its cities, Cordova, Toledo, Leon; what to him were the pagodas of Burmah and the lagoons of South Sea Islands? America was here and now. It seemed to him that all his life he had followed the ideals that other people, by their words or their writings, had instilled into him, and never the desires of his own heart. Always his course had been swayed by what he thought he should do and never by what he wanted with his whole soul to do. He put all that aside now with a gesture of impatience. He had lived always in the future, and the present always, always had slipped through his fingers. His ideals? He thought of his desire to make a design, intricate and beautiful, out of the myriad, meaningless facts of life: had he not seen also that the simplest pattern, that in which a man was born, worked, married, had children, and died, was likewise the most perfect? It might be that to surrender to happiness was to accept defeat, but it was a defeat better than many victories. He glanced quickly at Sally, he wondered what she was thinking, and then looked away again.

'I was going to ask you to marry me,' he said.

'I thought p'raps you might, but I shouldn't have liked to stand in your way.'

'You wouldn't have done that.'

'How about your travels, Spain and all that?'

'How d'you know I want to travel?'

Happy Endings

'I ought to know something about it. I've heard you and Dad talk about it till you were blue in the face.'

'I don't care a damn about all that.' He paused for an instant and then spoke in a low, hoarse whisper. 'I don't want to leave you! I can't leave you.'

She did not answer. He could not tell what she thought.

'I wonder if you'll marry me, Sally.'

She did not move and there was no flicker of emotion on her face, but she did not look at him when she answered.

'If you like.'

'Don't you want to?'

'Oh, of course I'd like to have a house of my own, and it's about time I was settling down.'

He smiled a little. He knew her pretty well by now, and her manner did not surprise him.

'But don't you want to marry *me*?'

'There's no one else I would marry.'

'Then that settles it.'

'Mother and Dad will be surprised, won't they?'

'I'm so happy.'

'I want my lunch,' she said.

'Dear!'

He smiled and took her hand and pressed it. They got up and walked out of the gallery. They stood for a moment at the balustrade and looked at Trafalgar Square. Cabs and omnibuses hurried to and fro, and crowds passed, hastening in every direction, and the sun was shining.

W. Somerset Maugham: *Of Human Bondage*

No longer alone

At the top of the hill he halted to look down upon the Garroch glen, with the end of Lower Loch Garroch a pool of gold in the late October sun. There was a sound behind him, and he turned to see a girl coming over the crest of the hill. It was Alison, and she was in a hurry, for she was hatless, and her cob was in a lather.

She swung herself to the ground with the reins looped round an arm.

'Oh, Jaikie!' she cried. 'Why did you leave without saying good-bye? I only heard by accident that you had gone, and I've had such a hustle to catch you up. Why did you do it?'

'I don't know,' said Jaikie. 'It seemed difficult to say good-bye to you, so I shirked it.' He spoke penitently, but there was no penitence in his face. That plain little wedge of countenace was so lit up that it was almost beautiful.

They sat down on a bank of withered heather and looked over the Garroch to the western hills.

'What fun we have had!' Alison sighed. 'I hate to think that it is over. I hate your going away.'

Jaikie did not answer. It was difficult for one so sparing of speech to find words equal to that sudden glow in his eyes.

'When are we going to meet again?' she asked.

'I don't know,' he said at last. 'But we are going to meet again. . . often . . . always.'

He turned, and he saw in her face that comprehension which needs no words.

They sat for a little, and then she rose. 'I must go back,' she said, 'or Aunt Hatty will be dragging the ponds for me.'

They shook hands, quite prosaically. He watched her mount and turn her horse's head to the Callowa, while he turned his own

Happy Endings

resolutely to the Garroch. He took a few steps and then looked back. The girl had not moved.

'*Dear Jaikie,*' she said, and the intervening space did not weaken the tenderness of the words. Then she put her horse into a canter, and the last he saw was a golden head disappearing over the brow of the hill.

He quickened his pace, and strode down into the Garroch valley with his mind in a happy confusion. Years later, when the two monosyllables of his name were famous in other circles than those of Rugby football, he was to remember that evening hour as a crisis in his life. For, as he walked, his thoughts moved towards a new clarity and a profound concentration . . . He was no longer alone. The seeker had found something infinitely precious. He had a spur now to endeavour, such endeavour as would make the common bustle of life seem stagnant. A force of high velocity had been unloosed on the world.

These were not Jaikie's explicit thoughts: he only knew that he was happy, and that he was glad to have no companion but Woolworth. He passed the shores of Lower Loch Garroch, and his singing scared the mallards out of the reeds. He came into the wide cup of the Garroch moss, shadowed by its sentinel hills, with the light of the Back House to guide him through the thickening darkness. But he was not conscious of the scene, for he was listening to the songs which youth was crooning in his heart.

John Buchan: *Castle Gay*

Molly Bloom's soliloquy

He said I was a flower of the mountain yes so we are flowers all a womans body yes that was one true thing he said in his life and the sun shines for you today yes that was why I liked him because I saw he understood or felt what a woman is and I knew I could always get round him and I gave him all the pleasure I could leading him on till

Happy Endings

he asked me to say yes and I wouldnt answer first only looked out over the sea and the sky I was thinking of so many things he didn't know of Mulvey and Mr Stanhope and Hester and father and old captain Groves and the sailors playing all birds fly and I say stoop and washing up dishes they called it on the pier and the sentry in front of the governors house with the thing round his white helmet poor devil half roasted and the Spanish girls laughing in their shawls and their tall combs and the auctions in the morning the Greeks and the Jews and the Arabs and the devil knows who else from all the ends of Europe and Duke street and the fowl market all clucking outside Larby Sharons and the poor donkeys slipping half asleep and the vague fellows in the cloaks asleep in the shade on the steps and the big wheels of the carts of the bulls and the old castle thousands of years old yes and those handsome Moors all in white and turbans like kings asking you to sit down in their little bit of a shop and Ronda with the old windows of the posadas glancing eyes a lattice hid for her lover to kiss the iron and the wine shops half open at night and the castanets and the night we missed the boat at Algeciras the watchman going about serene with his lamp and O that awful deep down torrent O and the sea the sea crimson sometimes like fire and the glorious sunsets and the figtrees in the Alameda gardens yes and all the queer little streets and pink and blue and yellow houses and the rose gardens and the jessamine and geraniums and cactuses and Gibraltar as a girl where I was a Flower of the mountain yes when I put the rose in my hair like the Andalusian girls used or shall I wear a red yes and how he kissed me under the Moorish wall and I thought well as well him as another and then I asked him with my eyes to ask again yes and then he asked me would I yes to say yes my mountain flower and first I put my arms around him yes and drew him down to me so he could feel my breasts all perfume yes and his heart was going like mad and yes I said yes I will Yes.

James Joyce: *Ulysses*

Happy Endings

he asked me to say yes and I wouldnt answer first only looked out over the sea and the sky I was thinking of so many things he didn't know of Mulvey and Mr Stanhope and Hester and father and old captain Groves and the sailors playing all birds fly and I say stoop and washing up dishes they called it on the pier and the sentry in front of the governors house with the thing round his white helmet poor devil half roasted and the Spanish girls laughing in their shawls and their tall combs and the auctions in the morning the Greeks and the Jews and the Arabs and the devil knows who else from all the ends of Europe and Duke street and the fowl market all clucking outside Larby Sharons and the poor donkeys slipping half asleep and the vague fellows in the cloaks asleep in the shade on the steps and the big wheels of the carts of the bulls and the old castle thousands of years old yes and those handsome Moors all in white and turbans like kings asking you to sit down in their little bit of a shop and Ronda with the old windows of the posadas glancing eyes a lattice hid for her lover to kiss the iron and the wine shops half open at night and the castanets and the night we missed the boat at Algeciras the watchman going about serene with his lamp and O that awful deep down torrent O and the sea the sea crimson sometimes like fire and the glorious sunsets and the figtrees in the Alameda gardens yes and all the queer little streets and pink and blue and yellow houses and the rose gardens and the jessamine and geraniums and cactuses and Gibraltar as a girl where I was a Flower of the mountain yes when I put the rose in my hair like the Andalusian girls used or shall I wear a red yes and how he kissed me under the Moorish wall and I thought well as well him as another and then I asked him with my eyes to ask again yes and then he asked me would I yes to say yes my mountain flower and first I put my arms around him yes and drew him down to me so he could feel my breasts all perfume yes and his heart was going like mad and yes I said yes I will Yes.

James Joyce: *Ulysses*